Living Loved
Living Free

Experience the freedom
of living in the Father's love,
through the finished
work of Jesus

by
CONNIE WITTER

D1453474

Living Loved, Living Free

DEDICATION

This book is dedicated to
my wonderful husband, Tony.

Thank you so much for loving and supporting
me throughout the writing of this book.

I appreciate and love you more than you know.

ACKNOWLEDGEMENTS

To all my wonderful friends in Christ who have faithfully attended the Bible Study and contributed to the writing of this book. I am so very thankful for your friendship and support.

I especially want to thank the staff of
Because of Jesus Ministries:

Nancy Bishop, Art Director:
your gift continues to amaze me;

Rose Karlebach, Editor:
you are gifted in so many ways;

Lisa Aldrich, Office Administrator and Web Design:
I can't thank you enough for all you do;

Wayne and Marsha Rivers, Audio/Video Directors:
you have both been such an encouragement
and blessing to me;

Sherry Hensley, Marketing:
thank you for reading through the manuscript,
and helping to spread the message of the
Good News we have in Jesus;

And Shannan Orr:
your help with distributing the resources of BOJ,
writing and artwork are very much appreciated.
You are a blessing!

Your encouragement and suggestions are valuable to me;
I love and appreciate you all very much!

TABLE OF CONTENTS

PART 6 AMAZING GRACE

PART 7 ABIDING IN HIS LOVE

PART 8 PERFECT LOVE CASTS OUT ALL FEAR

PART 9 A PLACE OF REST

PART 10 ETERNAL LOVE

Living Loved, Living Free was written from my own personal experience, learning to live in the Father's love. For many years of my Christian life I was held captive by the devil's lies which I know you've heard, too: "You're not good enough." "They're better than you." "Something is wrong with you." "You lack in some way." I believed these lies about myself and they kept me in bondage to fear, worry, condemnation, shame, and insecurity. Even though I was a daughter of the King, I lived like a fearful slave, trying to earn my Heavenly Father's blessing and approval instead of receiving it as a free gift of His grace. All my effort was spent trying to be like Jesus instead of embracing the truth that because of His gift of righteousness, I was already just like Him. I saw myself as lacking, instead of complete in Jesus. Because I really didn't know my Heavenly Father's amazing, unconditional, unchanging love, I wasn't enjoying the freedom that Jesus had purchased for me.

Within these pages is the truth the Holy Spirit revealed to me which has totally transformed my heart and my life. Each time I read through this manuscript, I am once again overwhelmed with the Good News of My Heavenly Father's love and grace toward me which has set my heart free. As I've learned to live in my Father's love, my heart has continually overflowed with love, joy, and the peace that passes all understanding. I now know how much He loves me and have put my trust in His love. I am living loved and living free!

I invite you to take this journey with me, and experience

this same freedom of living in the Father's love, through the finished work of Jesus. As we read Ephesians Chapters 1-3, you'll come to realize that only in Jesus can you find out *who you really are* and *what you are living for.* You'll come to know for yourself a love so great that it satisfies every desire and need of your heart.

This book was written to help you personally identify and expose the lies the devil has used to keep you captive, and to encourage you to live in your Heavenly Father's love where true freedom abounds. You'll discover the one lie the enemy tempts God's children to believe, and the one truth that has the power to set you completely free! Jesus made it possible for us to live in the truth of the Father's love, but for far too long we have believed our enemy's lies. While the symptoms are clear: discouragement, depression, worry, fear, resentment, frustration, anger, insecurity, condemnation and pride, it's time for freedom. It's time to begin agreeing with the One Who loves you. As you discover who you truly are in Jesus and come to believe it, you'll begin to live the glorious life He has always planned. You'll find true freedom in living loved by Him, and experience the abundant life that is your inheritance as a beloved child of the King. It is my prayer that you'll fill your heart with the truth, and you'll truly learn to live loved and live free!

LIVING LOVED, LIVING FREE

EPHESIANS 1:1-14 PERSONALIZED FROM
THE MESSAGE BIBLE

*Heavenly Father, what a blessing You are! You take me
to the high places of blessing in Jesus. Long before You
laid down earth's foundations, You had me in mind, had
settled on me as the focus of Your love, to be made whole
and holy by Your love. Long, long ago You decided to adopt
me into Your family through Jesus Christ. (What pleasure
You took in planning this!) You wanted me to enter into
the celebration of Your lavish gift-giving by the hand of
Your beloved Son. Because of the sacrifice of Jesus, His
blood poured out on the altar of the Cross, I have been set
free — free of the penalties and punishments chalked up by
my misdeeds. And not just barely free, either. Abundantly
free! You thought of everything, provided for everything
I could possibly need, letting me in on the plans You took
such delight in making. You set it all out before me in Jesus,
a long-range plan in which everything would be brought
together and summed up in Him.*

*For it's in You, Jesus, that I find out who I am and what I
am living for. Long before I first heard of You and got my
hopes up, You had Your eye on me, had designs on me for
glorious living, part of the overall purpose You are working
out in everything and everyone.*

*And it's in You, Jesus, that I, once I heard the truth and
believed it, found myself home free — signed, sealed, and
delivered by the Holy Spirit. This signet from You is the
first installment on what's coming, a reminder that I'll
receive everything You have planned for me,
a praising and glorious life.*

EPHESIANS 3:17-20 PERSONALIZED FROM THE NEW LIVING TRANSLATION AND AMPLIFIED BIBLE

[17]Jesus, make Your home in my heart as I believe and trust You. May my roots grow down deep into Your marvelous love and keep me strong. [18]May I have the power to understand, as all God's people should, how wide, how long, how high, and how deep Your love is for me. [19]May I experience Your love, Jesus, though it is too great to fully understand. Then I will be made complete with all the fullness of life and power that comes from You. [20]Now, according to Your power that is at work within me, You are able to carry out Your purpose for my life and do superabundantly, far over and above all that I dare ask or think — infinitely beyond my highest prayers, desires, thoughts, hopes, or dreams!

PART 1

CREATED TO BE LOVED

*Long before he laid down earth's foundations, he
had us in mind, had settled on us as the focus of his
love, to be made whole and holy by his love.*

EPHESIANS 1:4 MSG

Chapter 1

CREATED TO BE LOVED

³The Father ... has blessed us with every spiritual blessing in the heavenly realms because we are united with [Jesus]. NLT
⁴Long before he laid down earth's foundations, he had us in mind, had settled on us as the focus of his love, to be made whole and holy by His love.

EPHESIANS 1:3-4 MSG

Did you know that before God ever created the world, you were on His mind? He wanted sons and daughters that He could love. He settled on you as the focus of His love. Through making you one with Jesus, God planned to make your heart whole by His love. *Whole* means "to be complete; to lack nothing." It has always been God's plan for you to feel complete; for your heart to be whole; for you to lack nothing. He created you to find your identity and worth in His love for you. His plan was to fill every need in your heart with His love so that you would be completely satisfied and fulfilled in your relationship with Him. 1 John 4:8 says, *God is love.* You were created to be loved by Him.

Now you're probably asking, "If God is love and He created us to be made whole by His love, then why is the world in such a mess? Didn't God, in His love for us, promise us peace, love, and overflowing joy? Then why are there so many hurting people with broken hearts? And why do so many of God's people seem to be wandering in a wilderness of shame, confusion, fear, insecurity, depression and disappointment?" Those are excellent questions. Let's take a look into the word of God to find the answer.

In the beginning, God created man and woman. He loved them and His opinion of them was very good.

Genesis 1:26, 27, 31:

> *²⁶Then God said, "Let us make people in our image to be like ourselves." ²⁷So God created people in His own image... ³¹Then God looked over all he had made, and he saw that it was excellent in every way. NLT¹*

> *³¹And God saw everything that He had made, and behold, it was very good... and He approved it completely. AMP*

> *³¹God looked over everything he had made; it was so good, so very good! MSG*

When God looked at Adam and Eve He saw Himself. He had created them in His very own image and they were just like Him. As He lovingly admired His son and daughter, He said, *You are excellent in every way! You are so good, so very good! I approve of you completely!* He had a very good opinion of them. Adam and Eve were God's dream, and He created them to be the focus of His love.

Genesis 2:25:

> *²⁵Now, although Adam and his wife were both naked, neither of them felt any shame. NLT¹*

In the beginning, Adam and Eve's hearts were free from shame. They were free from any negative opinion about themselves or each other. They were free from any sense of lack. They had no difficulty receiving God's love into their hearts or believing His good opinion of them. They had His approval and acceptance, and it made them feel valuable and loved by Him. Every need of their heart was met and they lacked nothing. They felt complete in His love.

But something happened that changed the way Adam and Eve felt about themselves:

> Genesis 3:1-6: *¹Now the serpent was the shrewdest of all the creatures the Lord God had made. "Really?" he asked the woman, "Did God really say you must not eat any of the fruit in the garden?" ²"Of course we may eat it," the woman told him. ³"It's only the fruit from the tree at the center of the garden that we are not allowed to eat. God says we must not eat it or even touch it, or we will die." ⁴"You won't die!" the serpent hissed. ⁵"God knows that your eyes will be opened when you eat it. You will become just like God, knowing everything, both good and evil." ⁶The woman was convinced. The fruit looked so fresh and delicious, and it would make her so wise! So she ate some of the fruit. She also gave some to her husband, who was with her. Then he ate it, too. NLT[1]*

The devil devised a plan to separate Adam and Eve from their love relationship with God. He did this by deceiving them into believing three lies:

1. You can't trust what God says. What He says about you isn't true. (Verse 1)
2. You're not like God. You lack in some way. (Verse 5)
3. You need to do something to be like God. You need to fix yourself and your spouse.

The truth is that God loved Adam and Eve completely. They could trust Him because everything God says is true (Proverbs 30:5).

The truth is that they were made in God's image. They were already like God. They were complete in Him. They lacked nothing. (Genesis 1:26)

The truth is Eve *didn't need to do anything* to fix herself or her husband because they were already excellent in every way. They were very good just as God had said. (Genesis 1:31)

Unfortunately for the human race, Eve chose to believe the lies of the enemy. Because she doubted what God said about her, she experienced lack in her heart. This caused her to look outside of her relationship with God to make her heart feel complete. She tried to fix herself and Adam by eating from the tree of the knowledge of good and evil, and what was the end result?

Genesis 3:7:

> *At that moment, their eyes were opened, and they suddenly felt shame at their nakedness. NLT* [1]

Shame means:

> A painful emotion caused by consciousness of guilt or failure; judging yourself unworthy; unlovable; a negative opinion about yourself

The state of having lost the respect (or good opinion) of others

Shame entered into Adam and Eve's hearts, which had once been whole, complete, and filled with God's love. As a result, they immediately began to judge themselves and each other as bad, unworthy, and unlovable, so they hid from God. Because they exchanged the truth (God's good opinion of them) for the enemy's lies, their hearts were broken. As a result, sin and shame entered into the human race and it caused the hearts of everyone God created to be broken (Romans 5:12). Ever since Adam and Eve, the enemy has deceived all of us into believing these same three lies. Just like Eve, we've all gone outside of our relationship with God to get the needs of our hearts met, leaving us brokenhearted.

A *broken heart* is:

one that lacks peace, confidence, security, and joy. To be brokenhearted means "to be disheartened by circumstances; discouraged, depressed, defeated, or disappointed."

- Have you ever experienced a broken heart by believing the enemy's lies?
- Have you ever looked at your failures and felt shame in your heart?
- Have you ever judged yourself unworthy, unlovable, or had a negative opinion about yourself?
- Have you ever felt like you lost the good opinion of your Heavenly Father?

At one time or another, we've all fallen for the devil's lies and have experienced the feeling of shame in our hearts. Although shame may have created brokenness within your heart, your Heavenly Father had a plan before the foundation of the world to redeem you and heal your heart with His love. In **Genesis 3:15,** God spoke to the serpent and said, *"From now on, you and the woman will be enemies, and your offspring and her offspring will be enemies. He will crush your head, and you will strike his heel." NLT* [1] God prophesied of a Redeemer who would come from the womb of a woman and would crush the enemy's head. His name is Jesus.

1 John 3:8:

> [8] *"...the devil has sinned...from the beginning. The reason the Son of God was made manifest ...was to undo (destroy, loosen, and dissolve) the works [of] the devil." AMP*

The *works of the devil* is sin which creates shame in the hearts of God's children. Jesus destroyed the works of the devil by becoming the sacrifice needed to take away our sin and shame in order to make our hearts whole once again.

Jesus reconciled you back to the Father's good opinion so that you would never again have to live in shame. No matter what mistakes you and I may have made in our past, no matter what mistakes we may make today or in our future, our Heavenly Father's good opinion of us will never change because He now looks at us through the blood of Jesus.

Ephesians 1:3-4:

> *³All praise to God, the Father of our Lord Jesus Christ, who has blessed us with every spiritual blessing in the heavenly realms because we are united with Christ. ⁴Even before he made the world, God loved us and chose us in Christ to be holy and without fault in his eyes. NLT ²*

2 Corinthians 5:21:

> *²¹Christ did no wrong thing. But for our sake God put the blame for our wrong ways on Christ. So now God sees us as good, because we are in Christ. WE*

Read these verses again and think about the truth that is being revealed in them. How does your Heavenly Father see you because you are in Christ? What is His good opinion of you?

God created you to be loved by Him. He created you with the need in your heart for unconditional love that only He could fill. He knew you would fail by believing the lies of the enemy just like Adam and Eve. He knew your heart would feel shame and become broken, so before you were even born, He had a plan in place to redeem you through Jesus. His plan was to restore you back into His favor by cleansing you from all your sin through the blood of Jesus.

In the very same way He looked at Adam and Eve in the beginning, your Heavenly Father looks at you through the blood of Jesus and says:

My Beloved,
You are excellent in every way! You are
good, so very good, and I approve of you
completely! You are without fault in my
eyes because of your faith in my Son,
Jesus, and there is nothing you could ever
do to change My good opinion of you!
Your Heavenly Father

How does it make your heart feel to know that this is the way your Heavenly Father feels toward you? The devil will continue to tempt you with the same three lies he used on Eve, and these three lies can be summed up in this one lie: *You're not who God says you are.* The devil knows that if you believe him, you'll go outside of your relationship with Jesus to meet the needs of your heart, and your heart will be filled with shame and brokenness.

In Isaiah 61:1 and 2 Jesus said, *"...the Lord has anointed me to preach good news to the poor. He has sent me to bind up the brokenhearted, to proclaim freedom for the captives and release from darkness for the prisoners, ²to proclaim the year of the Lord's favor...." NIV*

Jesus came to make your heart whole with the Good News of God's love and acceptance. When you believe who you are in Christ, your heart is made whole and complete by His amazing love.

Chapter 2

LIVING LOVED

*⁴Long before he laid down earth's foundations,
he had us in mind, had settled on us as the focus of his love,
to be made whole and holy by his love.*

EPHESIANS 1:4 MSG

God created you with a deep need within your heart to be completely and unconditionally loved. The Greek word for God's love in Ephesians 1:4 is *agape*. (Strong's 26) Agape love places value on the person being loved regardless of their behavior. Unlike the kind of love the world offers which is conditional and based on your performance, agape (God's love) is an unconditional love that is not earned based on what you do, how you behave, or how you look. It is given freely by God based on who you are — the object of His affection.

Romans 5:8-9:

> *⁸But God showed his great love for us by sending Christ to die for us while we were still sinners.* NLT
>
> *⁹....We are now justified (acquitted, made righteous, and brought into right relationship with God) by Christ's blood.* AMP

You did nothing to earn or deserve God's love. God proved His unconditional love for you by sending Jesus to die for you when you were still a sinner. He loves you so much that He didn't leave you in your sin. When you put your faith in Jesus, He completely redeemed you by giving you a brand new identity. He didn't want you to identify yourself with your sin and failure so He changed your identity completely. He made you righteous in Christ. He wants your heart to be filled everyday with the truth of His great love for you!

Ephesians 3:17-19:

> *17Then Christ will make his home in your hearts as you trust in him. Your roots will grow down into God's love and keep you strong. 18And may you have the power to understand, as all God's people should, how wide, how long, how high, and how deep his love is. 19May you experience the love of Christ.... Then you will be made complete with all the fullness of life and power that comes from God. NLT 2*

Your heart is God's dwelling place. He created your heart with the need to be filled up with complete approval, complete acceptance, and to feel completely valued. God is love and He is the only One Who can truly meet every need of your heart and make your heart whole. Ephesians 3:17-19 teaches us that when we live in Christ's love we will truly feel complete and be filled with the fullness of life and power that comes from God.

The word *fullness* in this verse comes from the Greek word *pleroma*. It means "to fill up to completion." Romans 5:5 says, *God's love has been poured out in our hearts through the Holy Spirit. AMP* God's love fills us up completely.

Colossians 2:9-10:

> [9]*For in Christ lives all the fullness of God in a human body.* [10]*So you also are complete through your union with Christ....* NLT [2]

The fullness of God dwells in you because you are in Christ, and He is in you. You are just like Him. You are complete and you lack nothing in Him. You are completely loved, completely righteous, completely accepted, completely approved, completely capable, and a complete success in Him. It is this Good News that Jesus was sent to tell you (Isaiah 61:1-11).

And yet the devil is constantly trying to tempt you to look outside of Christ for your identity and worth. All of our hearts have been broken at one time or another because just like Adam and Eve, we have believed the lies of the enemy, and looked outside of Jesus to meet our need to be completely loved.

In Chapter 1, you learned that the three lies the devil tempted Eve with can be summed up in this one lie:

YOU'RE NOT WHO GOD SAYS YOU ARE

Let's look at those three lies again:

1. **You can't trust what God says** = *you're not who God says you are*

2. **You lack in some way** = *you're not who God says you are*

3. **You need to do something to fix yourself** = *you're not who God says you are*

If you believe any of the devil's lies, he has convinced you that *you're not who God says you are.*

For example:

LIES:	The Root of Every Lie	TRUTH:
You're not loved	= you're not who God says you are	John 15:9 Jesus says He loves you
You can't do it	= you're not who God says you are	Philippians 4:13 says you can do all things through Jesus
You're inadequate	= you're not who God says you are	Hebrews 13:21 says God has equipped you with everything you need to be a success
What if you fail?	= you're not who God says you are	Proverbs 16:3 says you are a success
You're not worthy	= you're not who God says you are	Col. 1:12-14 says Jesus has qualified you
They don't like you	= you're not who God says you are	Psalm 5:12 says God surrounds you with favor
You need to be productive to be valuable	= you're not who God says you are	1 Peter 1:18-19 says Jesus proved your value by paying for you with His blood
God isn't going to meet your needs	= you're not who God says you are	2 Corinthians 9:8 says all grace abounds toward you and God will abundantly supply your needs
You're not good enough	= you're not who God says you are	2 Corinthians 5:21 says you are the righteousness of God in Christ

The devil schemes every day to tempt you to believe this one lie. It may come at you in many different ways and through many different channels, but the root of every lie is always the same. If you believe that *you're not who God says you are,* then just like Adam and Eve, you'll look outside of your relationship with God to meet your sense of lack. When you do this, it will bring shame and brokenness into your heart, and it will affect your life in a negative way. This one lie of the devil is intended to keep you from experiencing the fullness of life that is found in the love of Jesus.

Romans 8:39:

> *No power in the sky above or in the earth below—indeed, nothing in all creation will ever be able to separate us from the love of God that is revealed in Christ Jesus our Lord. NLT [2]*

A REVELATION OF GOD'S LOVE FOR YOU IS REVEALED IN WHO YOU ARE IN CHRIST

Ephesians 1:11-14:

> *It's in Christ that we find out who we are and what we are living for. Long before we first heard of Christ and got our hopes up, he had his eye on us, had designs on us for glorious living, part of the overall purpose he is working out in everything and everyone. It's in Christ that you, once you heard the truth and believed it (this Message of your salvation), found yourselves home free — signed, sealed, and delivered by the Holy Spirit. This signet from God is the first installment on what's coming,*

a reminder that we'll get everything God has planned for us, a praising and glorious life. MSG

It is in Christ that you find out who you are and what you are living for. That is why the enemy is constantly trying to tempt you to believe that you're not who God says you are. He knows that if you ever discover who you really are in Christ and believe it, you'll begin to live the glorious life that God has always planned for you. You'll find true freedom in living loved by Him.

TWO WAYS TO LIVE

LIVING UNLOVED = BONDAGE

I lack in some way
I am not who God says I am
I am not loved

BELIEVING LIES

LIVING LOVED = FREEDOM

I am complete in Christ
I am who God says I am

Jesus, I know
You love me!

BELIEVING TRUTH

WHEN YOU BELIEVE YOUR HEAVENLY FATHER AND HIS OPINION OF YOU IN CHRIST, YOU ARE LIVING LOVED BY HIM

I have come to realize that whenever I feel my heart becoming sad or discouraged, the devil is tempting me to believe this lie: *I am not who God says I am.* The negative emotions I am experiencing indicate that I am feeling lack in my heart and am looking somewhere other than Jesus to be completely loved.

Recently, my heart felt sad concerning my relationship with my two grown sons. For most of their lives my sons have needed me on a pretty regular basis. Now that they are adults and living on their own, they don't need me as much as they used to. Because I hadn't heard from either of them in over a week, my heart began feeling sad as I thought, *Well, I guess they don't need me anymore.* As I recognized this sense of lack, I turned my thoughts to the Lord and said, "Lord, I'm feeling really sad. I feel like my boys don't need me anymore. Show me the truth that will set my heart free."

As I looked toward the Lord, His words of love flooded my soul. I heard Him say, "Connie, you are looking to your boys to meet the need in your heart to feel valuable. I proved your value by paying for you with My blood. You don't need anybody else in this world to fill that need in your heart but Me."

As the Lord spoke to me, I realized that I had been looking to my boys to determine my worth. Their need for me meant that I was valuable and it gave me a purpose in the world. But as I sat in the presence of the Lord, letting Him fill my heart with His love, the lie of the enemy was exposed and the truth of who I am in Jesus became very real to me. I responded, "Lord, I know You love me because You proved my value by laying Your life down for me. Thank You Lord, for filling that need in my heart and making me whole. My purpose for being here is to be loved by You and to love others with Your love."

The emotions you experience in your heart are an indicator of what you are believing. Be conscious of how your heart feels; realize that if you are experiencing negative emotions, the devil is tempting you to believe that you are not who God says you are. Turn to Jesus and ask Him to reveal the truth of who you are in Him. Let Him fill your heart with His great love; there is nothing else in the world that can completely satisfy your soul. You are complete in Jesus; created to be made whole, living loved by Him.

Chapter 3

ASK, LISTEN, RESPOND

*16 May He grant you out of the rich treasury of His glory to
be strengthened and reinforced with mighty power in the
inner man by the [Holy] Spirit...17 May Christ through
your faith [actually] dwell...in your hearts! May you be
rooted deep in love and founded securely on love, 18 that you
may have the power and be strong to apprehend and grasp
with all saints [God's devoted people, the experience of that
love] what is the breadth and length and height and depth
[of it]; 19 [that you may really come] to know [practically,
through experience for yourselves] the love of Christ, which
far surpasses mere knowledge;...
that you may be filled [through all your being] unto
all the fullness of God....*

*20 Now to Him Who, by... the [action of His] power that
is at work in us, is able to [carry out His purpose and] do
superabundantly, far over and above all that we [dare]
ask or think [infinitely beyond our highest prayers, desires,
thoughts, hopes, or dreams] —21 To Him be glory in the
church and in Christ Jesus throughout all generations
forever and ever! Amen.*

EPHESIANS 3:16-21 AMP

What a powerful passage of Scripture! These verses show
me that everything my heart desires is found in knowing
the love Jesus has for me. The fullness of God and being
able to experience His life and power at work in my heart

has everything to do with me learning to live in His love. As you and I abide in His love, He is able to bring to pass His purpose for our lives and do superabundantly, far over and above our highest prayers, desire, thoughts, hopes or dreams.

1 Corinthians 14:1:

> *¹Go after a life of love as if your life depended on it— because it does.* MSG

> *¹**Eagerly pursue** and seek to acquire [this] love [make it your aim, your great quest].* AMP

The word *love* in this verse is *agape*. It is the unconditional, unfailing love of Jesus. This verse makes it very clear to me that my very life depends on me knowing and believing the love that God has for me. This love is found in Christ, and understanding this love has become my life's passion and my great quest. I want to think, act and love like Jesus. I want His life and power working in me and to experience the fullness of life that is found in living loved by Him. Because of this great desire, I asked the Lord, "How do I gain a deeper revelation of Your love? How do I learn to live loved by You?"

In response to my question I heard the Lord say, *"Ask, listen, and respond."* He then showed me this truth very clearly in His Word. I realized that this is how all revelation from God comes into a person's heart.

ASK

Inspired by the Holy Spirit, Ephesians 3:16 shows the Apostle Paul praying that you would be strengthened by the Holy Spirit to believe the love that Jesus has for you. The Holy Spirit is the One who gives you a revelation of who you are in Jesus and then empowers you to believe it.

Ephesians 1:16-18:

> ¹⁶*I have not stopped giving thanks for you, remembering you in my prayers.* ¹⁷ *I keep asking that the God of our Lord Jesus Christ, the glorious Father, may give you the Spirit of wisdom and revelation, so that you may know him better.* ¹⁸*I pray also that the eyes of your heart may be enlightened in order that you may know the hope to which he has called you, the riches of his glorious inheritance in the saints. NIV*

Jesus said in Luke 11:9,10,13:

> ⁹*So I say to you,* **ask and keep on asking** *and it shall be given you; seek and keep on seeking and you shall find; knock and keep on knocking and the door shall be opened to you.* ¹⁰***For everyone who asks and keeps on asking receives;*** *and he who seeks and keeps on seeking finds; and to him who knocks and keeps on knocking, the door shall be opened.* ¹³*If you then, evil as you are, know how to give good gifts...to your children, how much more will your heavenly Father give the Holy Spirit* **to those who ask and continue to ask Him***! AMP*

James 4:2:

> ²*You do not have, because you do not* **ask God***. NIV*

LISTEN

In Proverbs 4:20-22 God says:

> *²⁰My child, pay attention to what I say.* **Listen** *carefully to my words.* *²¹Don't lose sight of them. Let them penetrate deep into your heart, ²² for they bring life to those who find them, and healing to their whole body.* NLT

RESPOND

In Proverbs 22:17-19 God says:

> *¹⁷Listen...to the words of the wise, and apply your mind to my knowledge; ¹⁸ For it will be pleasant if you keep them in your mind [believing them]; your lips will be accustomed to [confessing] them. ¹⁹ So that your trust (belief, reliance, support, and confidence) may be in the Lord....* AMP

ASK, LISTEN, RESPOND

When I read these verses in the Bible it helps me to understand how a revelation of God's love and the freedom He offers in Christ is available to each of us if we will simply **ask**, **listen** and **respond** to what Jesus has done for us.

ASK: For so many years of my Christian life, I looked to others to teach me the truth. What I didn't realize is that Jesus has always wanted me to look to Him for the Truth. While God does use pastors and teachers to share His Word with us, He wants us to look to Him for revelation and understanding. That's why He gave us the Holy Spirit, the One who leads us into all truth when we ask Him. My journey to freedom began and continues to this day with this simple prayer: "Lord, show me the truth that will set me free." I continue to ask for a deeper revelation of who I am in Christ and His great love for me. I know that true freedom is found in living loved by Him.

LISTEN: When I began to ask for a revelation of His love, I began to hear the Holy Spirit speak to me through God's word. The Scriptures opened up to me like never before. Instead of seeing scripture as a set of laws that I needed to try to live up to, I began to see Jesus and who I am in Him. His love became very real to me as the Holy Spirit illuminated what Jesus had already accomplished for me on the cross. In addition to that, He gave me the power to believe it.

RESPOND: As I looked to Jesus, and received His love, I was empowered by the Holy Spirit to let go of the lies I believed and to truly believe Jesus. I responded to His word by continually agreeing with Him. My lips became accustomed to saying the same thing I heard my Father say about me and my family. As I did this, my heart overflowed with thanksgiving and His words of love set my heart free. As I have continued in this journey, I have become very aware that I need a daily revelation of who I am in Jesus and His great love for me. Yesterday's manna won't do. Every day the devil looks for an opportunity to tempt me to believe that I am not who God says I am. Each time I am tempted, I must look to Jesus for the revelation and strength to believe Him instead of the enemy's lies.

For example, just the other day I found myself becoming very frustrated while working on this manuscript because it just wasn't flowing. I had already spent hours working on it and felt like I had accomplished absolutely nothing. I felt like God wasn't helping me. Even though I had asked Him to help me, He seemed so far away. So I turned to Him and asked, "Lord, where are You? I asked You to help me, but You're not helping me." No sooner had I asked, when I recognized that I was believing a lie because of the negative feeling of frustration I was experiencing in my heart.

Once again, **I asked**, "Lord, show me the truth. Set my heart free." Gently and sweetly, the Lord showed me that while I was waiting on Him to help me, He was waiting on me to agree with who I am in Jesus. He had already given me everything I needed to successfully write this manuscript.

Rather than continue to be frustrated, **I listened** as He spoke His words of love to me and reminded me one more time of who I am in Jesus. The Holy Spirit reminded me of Hebrews 13:21 which says, *I am equipped through Christ with everything I need to carry out His will.* He also brought to my mind Isaiah 61:1 and 1 John 2:20, which say *I am anointed in Christ to open up the eyes of the blind and set the captives free,* and Philippians 4:13, *I can do all things through Christ who strengthens me.*

Responding to the Lord's encouraging words of love, I said, "Thank You, Jesus, for equipping me with everything I need to carry out Your will. I have Your wisdom, Your strength, and Your anointing to write this manuscript. I am qualified and anointed to set the captives free because You live in me." As I responded to His truth by agreeing with what He said about me, I was empowered by the Holy Spirit to put my full confidence and trust in Him. Afterwards, I sat down and wrote the end of this chapter, the words flowing out of me like rivers of living water.

Learning to live loved is a daily journey. Your very life depends on becoming established in the love of Jesus and understanding who you truly are in Him. Jesus longs for an intimate relationship with you. He is waiting for you to **ask, listen** and **respond** to Him. So bring the cares and needs of your heart to Him, and ask Him to reveal the truth of His great love for you. Listen as He exposes the lies of the devil and enlightens your heart to who you truly are in Jesus. Then respond to Him with a heart of thanksgiving. As you do, you'll find your heart being strengthened by the Holy Spirit to believe that you are truly loved, and you'll experience the fullness of life that God has always planned for you.

PART 2

THE FIGHT FOR YOUR HEART

[17]May Christ through your faith [actually] dwell (settle down, abide, make His permanent home) in your hearts! May you be rooted deep in love and founded securely on love, [18]that you may have the power and be strong to apprehend and grasp with all the saints [God's devoted people, the experience of that love] what is the breadth and length and height and depth [of it]; [19][that you may really come] to know [practically, through experience for yourselves] the love of Christ, which far surpasses mere knowledge [without experience]; that you may be filled [through all your being] unto all the fullness of God [may have the richest measure of the divine Presence, and become a body wholly filled and flooded with God Himself]!

[20]Now to Him Who, by (in consequence of) the [action of His] power that is at work within us, is able to [carry out His purpose and] do superabundantly, far over and above all that we [dare] ask or think [infinitely beyond our highest prayers, desires, thoughts, hopes, or dreams] — [21]To Him be glory in the church and in Christ Jesus throughout all generations forever and ever.
Amen (so be it).

EPHESIANS 3:17-21 AMP

Chapter 4

THE FIGHT FOR YOUR HEART

*17 May Christ through your faith [actually] dwell (settle
down, abide, make His permanent home) in your hearts!
May you be rooted deep in love
and founded securely on love.*
EPHESIANS 3:17 AMP

By the inspiration of the Holy Spirit the Apostle Paul
prayed that through your faith, Jesus would dwell and
abide in your heart and you would become rooted deeply
and securely in His love.

The word *heart* in Ephesians 3:17 comes from the Greek
word *kardia (Strong's 2588)*. According to *Strong's Concordance*
it means, "your thoughts, your feelings; your mind." The
Lexical Aids to the New Testament defines it as "the very seat
of your will."

Your heart is your mind, thoughts, and emotions. It is
where you decide what you believe. Often the beliefs of
your heart are established by what you've experienced in
life, what you've been taught, or how you've been treated.
In Ephesians 3:17 we see the Apostle Paul praying that the
beliefs of your heart would be centered in Christ and what
He has accomplished for you. He prayed that your mind,
your thoughts, and your emotions would be filled with the
truth of who you are in Jesus and His great love for you.

Romans 10:10:

> *¹⁰For it is with your heart that you believe.... NIV*

Are you aware that what you truly believe about God, Jesus, prayer, your spouse, your children, success, finances, righteousness, etc., is stored in your heart? In every area of your life you either believe the truth that God says about you or the lies of the devil. In the areas of your heart where you believe the devil's lies, they will bring forth shame, fear, and disappointment. In the areas of your heart where you believe the truth that God says about you, they will bring forth His glory.

Look back at the heart diagram and let's use your weight

as an example. If you believe the devil's lies and your heart belief is that *I can't control myself,* or *I'm a failure in this area,* or *I need food* (to meet an emotional need), then you'll struggle with weight all your life, feeling shame and disappointment with yourself. But if you truly believe down deep in your heart that what God says is true about you, such as *I have self-control. I am a healthy person. I don't need food* (to meet an emotional need) *because I know He loves me,* then you'll experience the glory of God in this area of your life and you'll maintain a healthy weight.

Let's take a look at another area: finances, for example. If you believe the devil's lies and the belief of your heart is that you lack, you'll be reluctant to give and bless others, you'll be discontent, make poor financial decisions, and you'll never feel like you have enough. As a result of these beliefs, you'll experience shame, fear, and disappointment in this area of your life. But if you believe down deep in your heart that what God says about you is true (regardless of what you may be experiencing in your life right now) you will think, *I am abundantly blessed because of Jesus. Lord, Your grace abounds toward me and I have more than enough to meet my needs. I am a good steward of what You have given me.* Then you'll freely give, be content and happy, make wise financial decisions and live in the abundant blessings of God. You'll experience peace and glorify God in this area of your life.

WHAT YOU BELIEVE IN YOUR HEART IS WHAT YOU'LL EXPERIENCE IN YOUR LIFE

Proverbs 23:7: *As [a man] thinks in his heart, so is he.* AMP

What you believe about yourself down deep in your heart will manifest in your life. Although I've been a Christian my entire life, it was not until I was twenty four years old that I truly began to experience the fullness of life that Jesus died to give me. For many years of my life I felt lack in almost every area because I believed the devil's lies. My heart belief about myself was that I lacked and that is exactly what I experienced. I lacked confidence, peace, joy, love, finances, favor, friendships, security, satisfaction and fulfillment because the belief of my heart was determining the fruit of my life.

Proverbs 27:19:

19As the water reflects the face, so the heart reflects the person. HCSB

MY LIFE REFLECTED THE BELIEFS OF MY HEART

The transformation in my life really started when I began to devote my heart, my mind, and my thoughts to Jesus. I began to continually think on the truth of who I am in Him and talk to Him daily about what He said about me. My mind began to be filled with thoughts like this: *Jesus, I know You love me because You died to make me righteous in You. Thank You for surrounding me with favor as a shield. I know You love me, Lord, because You approve of me. I am abundantly blessed because of You.* God's word began to penetrate deep within my heart and my heart beliefs started changing to those of abundance. As they did, my sense of lack disappeared, and what God said about me began to manifest in my life. I began to experience an abundance of peace, joy, friendships, favor, finances, as I became secure in the love of Jesus. The same is true for you. As you get your mind on Jesus, you'll find your heart becoming full of life. Any death in your soul will dissipate in the light of Jesus and you'll feel alive and free. You'll experience your heart being filled with the fullness of God.

THE FIGHT FOR YOUR HEART

God has an amazing plan for your life, but be aware that there is a fight going on for your heart. You are part of a royal race, chosen by God to receive His love and be like Him on the earth.

1 Peter 2:9:

> *⁹You are a chosen race, a royal priesthood, a dedicated nation, [God's] own purchased, special people, that you may set forth the wonderful deeds and display the virtues and perfections of Him Who called you out of darkness into His marvelous light. AMP*

As young children we love royal adventure stories where a princess is rescued by a handsome prince, or a young man overcomes evil, saves the princess, and becomes a king. These stories appeal to us because we are part of the royal family of God, and we want to take our rightful place in His kingdom.

It is interesting to note that in all of these stories there is always an evil person who lies to the prince or princess' heart in order to distract them from their royal destiny. You too, have an enemy — the devil — and he is constantly trying to convince you that: *You're not complete; you lack in some way. You're not who God says you are.*

There are two fighting for your heart. Jesus, the One Who loves you, is waiting for you to turn toward Him and invite Him to fill your heart with His words of love. The enemy however, doesn't need an invitation, and he begins his plan to fill your heart with lies from the moment you are born.

John 10:10:

> [10] *The thief comes only in order to steal and kill and destroy. I came that they may have and enjoy life and have it in abundance to the full, until it overflows.* AMP

The devil's plan for your heart and life is to steal, kill, and destroy, but Jesus' plan is that you enjoy life and have it in abundance! This verse clearly shows you that there are two plans for your life. Whomever you choose to believe down deep in your heart will determine the course of your life.

Proverbs 4:20-23:

> [20] *My child, pay attention to what I say. Listen carefully to my words.* [21] *Don't lose sight of them. Let them penetrate deep into your heart,* [22] *for they bring life to those who find them, and healing to their whole body.* [23] *Guard your heart above all else, for **it determines the course of your life**.* NLT [2]

Proverbs 4:23:

> [23] *Carefully guard your thoughts because they are the source of true life.* CEV

In these verses your Heavenly Father is admonishing you to pay attention to what He has to say and to listen carefully to the promises of His word. Don't allow yourself to be distracted by the devil's lies, or even what anyone else has to say. Let God's words penetrate deep within your heart. This means to think deeply about what He says and let His word become the center of who you are and the core of what you believe. True abundant life is experienced when the belief of your heart has nothing to do with what you feel, hear, or see, but everything to do with who you are in Jesus and what God says is true about you. Circumstances are subject to change, but the truth of who you are in Jesus remains the same.

When you believe God's words of love to be true, you'll find that they will bring life and health to you. The word *life* in verse 22 comes from the Hebrew words *chay* and *chayah* which mean, "to give promise, to restore, and to make whole." (*Strong's 2421*) The words that God speaks are alive and full of power (Hebrews 4:12). When you keep them in the center of your heart by keeping your thoughts on who you are in Christ, they will bring the manifestation of God's promises into every area of your life.

The word *health* in verse 22 comes from the Hebrew word *marpe (Strong's 4832)* which means "a medicine or a cure, deliverance, and healing." The word health is also derived from the Hebrew word *rapha* which is a word that describes God Himself, and means "to heal; a physician who thoroughly makes one whole." (*Strong's 7495*)

This is why God said in verse 23 that above everything you do in life **guard your heart**. The thoughts you allow into your heart will become what you believe, and those heart beliefs will affect your life in either a positive or negative way. Out of the beliefs of your heart will come the issues of your life. This is why you have two fighting for your heart. Each one wants you to devote your thoughts to their words and believe them down deep in your heart because whoever you choose to believe is whose plan will come to pass in your life. The devil's plan is to steal your joy and peace so that your heart is filled with shame, insecurity and fear. Jesus came to fill your heart with His love so that you could enjoy life and have it in abundance, to the full, till it overflows with peace, joy, love, security and blessing!

JESUS IS THE ONE WHO LOVES YOU

Jesus desperately wants you to bring your heart to Him and let Him fill your mind and thoughts with His words of love. He wants you to guard your heart from the lies of the enemy and choose to believe Him instead. If you desire to live in the fullness of life that Jesus came to give you, you must decide that you are done believing the enemy's lies, turn your heart to Jesus, and say, "Jesus, My heart belongs to You. Show me the lies of the devil that I have believed and help me to believe what You say about me. Help me to live in Your love."

Chapter 5

BREAKING FREE FROM
THE ENEMY'S LIES

*³But now I am fearful, lest that even as the serpent
beguiled Eve by his cunning, so your minds may be
corrupted and seduced from wholehearted and
sincere and pure devotion to Christ.*

2 CORINTHIANS 11:3 AMP

Inspired by the Holy Spirit, the Apostle Paul warned you in this scripture of the devil's plan to deceive your heart using the exact same lies he used on Eve. Although you've been told by Jesus that you are very good and that He approves of you completely, the Apostle Paul feared that in the very same way Eve was deceived, the devil would try to deceive you into believing that you're not good enough and that you're not who God says you are. Paul feared that your mind would be corrupted and your heart would be turned away from your pure devotion to Jesus.

John 8:44:

⁴⁴[T]he Devil... was a murderer from the beginning and has always hated the truth. There is no truth in him. When he lies, it is consistent with his character, for he is a liar and the father of lies. NLT²

1 Peter 5:8-9:

> [8]*Stay alert! Watch out for your great enemy, the devil. He prowls around like a roaring lion, looking for someone to devour.* [9]*Stand firm against him, and be strong in your faith.* NLT [2]

Ephesians 6:16:

> [16]*Above all, taking the shield of faith with which you will be able to quench all the fiery darts of the wicked one.* NKJV

THE AUTHOR OF ALL LIES IS THE DEVIL!

The fiery darts that the devil throws at you are his lies, intended to penetrate deep within your heart so that you will be in bondage to fear, insecurity and shame. The devil's only power is deception and he knows that if he can get you to agree with his lies, then you'll experience his plan for your life. 1 Peter 5:8-9 tells you to stay alert and be aware of your great enemy's plan to devour you with his lies. Guard your heart by resisting him and standing firm in your faith.

THE SYMPTOMS OF THE DEVIL'S LIES ARE NEGATIVE EMOTIONS

In order to guard your heart from the enemy's lies, you must first recognize when you're being tempted to believe a lie. Remember: **every lie the devil throws at you produces negative emotions.**

LIES PRODUCE NEGATIVE EMOTIONS

condemnation	jealousy
discouragement	guilt
fear	self-loathing
shame	frustration
disappointment	resentment
confusion	low-self image
sadness	judgement
depression	pride
worry	doubt
offense	anxiety
anger insecurity	restlessness

Have you ever heard these lies?

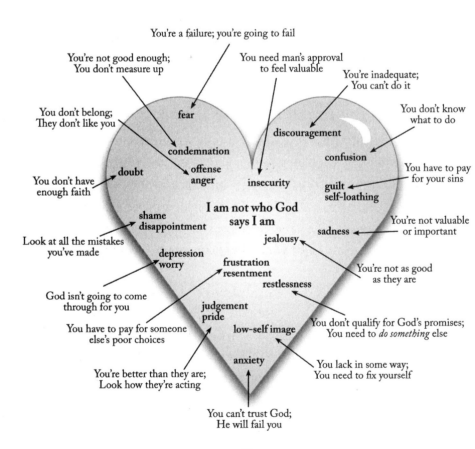

You're a failure; you're going to fail

You're not good enough;
You don't measure up

You need man's approval
to feel valuable

You're inadequate;
You can't do it

You don't belong;
They don't like you

You don't know
what to do

fear

discouragement

condemnation

confusion

You don't have
enough faith

doubt

offense
anger

insecurity

guilt
self-loathing

You have to pay
for your sins

I am not who God
says I am

shame
disappointment

sadness

You're not valuable
or important

Look at all the mistakes
you've made

jealousy

You're not as good
as they are

depression
worry

frustration
resentment

restlessness

God isn't going to come
through for you

judgement
pride

You have to pay for someone
else's poor choices

low-self image

You don't qualify for God's promises;
You need to do something else

anxiety

You lack in some way;
You need to fix yourself

You're better than they are;
Look how they're acting

You can't trust God;
He will fail you

The Bible makes it very clear that anxiety, condemnation, sadness, worry, guilt, discouragement, depression, fear, offense, bitterness, contention, pride, confusion, unrest, insecurity, judgmental thoughts toward someone and anger are all symptoms of believing the devil's lies. (See Ephesians 4:26-27; James 3:14-16; and 2 Timothy 2:25-26.)

Each time you agree with the lies of the enemy, his fiery darts are able to penetrate your heart and create emotional wounds that bring disappointment and heartache into your life. These lies always produce negative emotions. You will know when you're being tempted to believe a lie by how it makes your heart feel. When you find yourself experiencing negative emotions in your heart, be aware that the enemy is tempting you to believe a lie and turn your heart and thoughts back to Jesus.

A RECENT EXAMPLE

My most recent experience with this occurred just the other day as I was writing this book. The devil came once again to try and tempt me to quit by throwing his lies at my heart. Just like the Apostle Paul warned me in 2 Corinthians 11:2-3, the devil was trying to corrupt my mind so that my heart would be turned away from my pure devotion to Jesus.

I began to feel sad and discouraged, and wasn't quite sure why, but the symptoms were loud and clear. **It's at these moments that I have learned that if I want to live free, I must take my heart to Jesus and allow Him to shine the light of His truth on any darkness in my soul.** So while

I was driving to pick up my girls from school, I talked to Jesus. "Lord, I'm feeling sad and discouraged about writing this book. Show me the lie that I'm believing and help me to believe You." I recognized that the devil was tempting me to believe these particular lies: *It's too hard to write this book. It won't make a difference anyway, so why waste your time. It won't be any good or help anyone, so go do something else.*

So, I said, "Lord, I know this is not the truth, but it's how I feel at this moment, and honestly I feel like quitting. Strengthen me by Your grace." Thank goodness that Jesus is so faithful to run to our assistance when we humbly turn to Him in our moment of weakness! (Hebrews 2:18) He strengthened me once again with the promises of His word. As I surrendered the devil's lies to the truth of God's word, I found myself encouraged, and began to thank Him for His promises to me. I resisted the devil by saying, "Devil, you're a liar and a deceiver. My heart belongs to Jesus and I choose to believe Him." I continued, "Thank You, Lord, that You are causing my thoughts to be agreeable to Your will and everything I put my hand to will prosper and succeed" (Proverbs 16:3). "You create in me the desire and power to carry out Your will for my life" (Philippians 2:13). "You have anointed me to share and publish the Good News and Your word does not return void" (Isaiah 61:1-2; 1 John 2:20; Isaiah 55:11).

What I just shared is what it looks like to guard your heart from the enemy's lies, and to fill it with the truth. Without fail, every time I turn my heart to Jesus and allow

Him to fill my thoughts with His truth, I am set free from the devil's lies and their effect on my heart. Once more, the devil tried to deceive me with his lies so that I would quit and give up. He loves to distract us with busyness so that we won't accomplish what God has called us to do. That was his plan for me that day, and it would have come to pass if I had chosen to believe his lies.

The same is true for you. When you look to Jesus and allow Him to expose the lies and replace them with His truth, you'll find yourself experiencing God's plan and purpose for your life.

JESUS HAS COME TO RESCUE YOU AND SET YOUR HEART FREE FROM EVERY LIE OF THE ENEMY WITH THE TRUTH OF HIS LOVE

Jesus wants you to live free from fear. He wants you to live free from a low self image; free from insecurity; free from anxiety, discouragement, depression and every single negative emotion that keeps you in bondage.

Colossians 1:12-14:

> *[12]Always thanking the Father... [13]for he has rescued us from the one who rules in the kingdom of darkness and he has brought us into the Kingdom of his dear son. [14]God has purchased our freedom with his blood, and has forgiven all our sins. NLT[1]*

Isn't it wonderful to be part of a real adventure story? Jesus has rescued you from the devil's kingdom filled with darkness and lies. He's brought you into His kingdom, full of light and love. He has forgiven all your sins and made you righteous by purchasing your freedom with His blood. So guard your heart above everything else that you do. Don't let the devil corrupt your mind with his lies. Recognize the symptoms. When your heart feels a negative emotion, turn to Jesus and ask Him to help you believe the truth. Let Him fill your heart with the truth of His love, and you'll see yourself living in the freedom that He purchased for you.

Chapter 6

AGREE WITH THE ONE WHO LOVES YOU

*¹The spirit of the Lord God is upon me, because the Lord
has anointed... me to preach... good tidings to... the
poor.... He has sent me to... heal the brokenhearted, to
proclaim liberty to the... captives and the opening of
the prison... to those who are bound, ²To proclaim the
acceptable year of the Lord [the year of His favor].*

ISAIAH 61:1-2 AMP

In Isaiah 61 above, Jesus said that He came to heal your
heart with the Good News of His love and acceptance. Jesus
came to tell you the Good News to set your heart free. He
came to heal the broken places of your heart that were caused
by believing the lies of the enemy.

**LISTEN TO THE WORDS OF JESUS IN JEREMIAH 31:3,
11 AND 14 (PARAPHRASED BY THE AUTHOR)**

*³I have loved you with an everlasting love, with
everlasting kindness I have drawn you to myself
and continued my faithfulness to you. ¹¹I have
ransomed you and redeemed you from the hand
of your enemy. ¹⁴I will fully satisfy your soul with
abundance. I will satisfy you with my goodness."*

Jesus paid for you with His blood. He ransomed and
redeemed you from the hand of your enemy. The devil no
longer has any right to your heart; your heart now belongs
only to Jesus.

Before you accepted Jesus as your Savior, you were a sinner. There was something wrong with you. When you accepted Jesus however, your identity was changed. You became complete in Him (Colossians 2:9-10). You were made righteous. The devil used to be able to use your sins against you and tell you that you don't measure up because of your failures, but not anymore. Jesus took care of the sin problem. By His one sacrifice, all your sins were forgiven and you were made perfect in Him forever (Hebrews 10:14).

Jesus loves you with an extravagant, unfailing love and He wants your heart to be completely devoted to Him. He is the One Who loves you; His desire is to set your heart free with His love. He wants to satisfy your soul with abundance, and to fill your life with His goodness. He wants you to be rooted and secure in His love so that you might experience the fullness of life He has for you. He is waiting for you to give Him your heart (your thoughts and emotions) so that His words of love can bring healing and wholeness to your soul.

So how do you give your heart to the One Who loves you? How do you allow Him to dwell and make His permanent home in your heart so that you can be made whole with His love? Let's look at Ephesians 3:17 again:

> *17May Christ **through your faith** [actually] dwell (settle down, abide, make his permanent home) in your hearts. May you be rooted deep in love and founded securely on love. AMP*

This scripture says that it is through your faith that Jesus is able to fill your mind, thoughts, and emotions with His love. The word faith in this verse comes from the Greek words *pistis* and *peitho. Strong's Concordance* defines *faith* (*Strong's 4102*) as:

- ◈ Reliance upon Jesus for salvation
- ◈ To trust and believe
- ◈ To agree with

This verse says that when you believe Jesus by agreeing with what He says about you, you'll experience His love in the depths of your heart. He'll indwell your mind, your thoughts and your feelings and you'll experience freedom. You'll live free from fear, insecurity, unforgiveness, resentment, worry, doubt, offense, discouragement, and confusion when you agree with the One Who loves you. Just as the lies of the devil produce negative emotions within your heart, the truth Jesus says produces positive emotions within your heart. You can always know when you are listening to the truth by how it makes your heart feel.

In John 8:31-32 Jesus said:

> *³¹If you abide in my word… you are truly my disciple. ³²And you will know the Truth, and the Truth will set you free.* AMP

In John 16:33 Jesus said:

> *³³I have told you these things, so that in Me you may have **perfect [peace]** and **confidence.*** AMP

In John 15:11 Jesus said:

> *¹¹I have told you these things, that My joy and delight may be in you, and that **your joy** and **gladness** may be of full measure and complete and overflowing.* AMP

JESUS IS THE TRUTH

Jesus is the Truth, and every word He speaks is truth. When you agree with what He says about you, your heart will be full of perfect peace and confidence in Him. His words of love produce overflowing joy in your heart.

Psalm 119:162:

> *162I rejoice in your word like one who finds a great treasure. NLT¹*

Every day we are either agreeing with the enemy's lies, or we are agreeing with the One Who loves us. Who we agree with determines the condition of our heart and ultimately the fruit of our lives. So let's look for a moment at the words that Jesus speaks to us through God's Word.

JESUS' WORDS ARE TRUTH

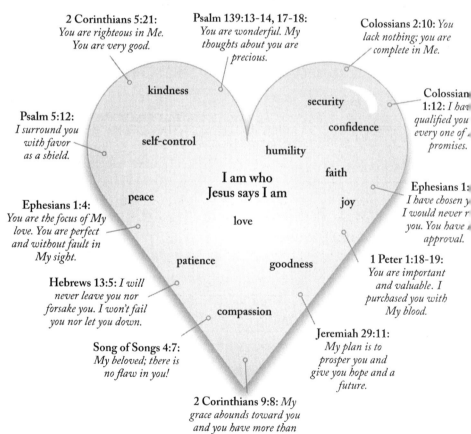

2 Corinthians 5:21:
You are righteous in Me. You are very good.

Psalm 139:13-14, 17-18:
You are wonderful. My thoughts about you are precious.

Colossians 2:10: *You lack nothing; you are complete in Me.*

Psalm 5:12:
I surround you with favor as a shield.

Colossians 1:12: *I have qualified you every one of promises.*

Ephesians 1:4:
You are the focus of My love. You are perfect and without fault in My sight.

Ephesians 1:
I have chosen y I would never r you. You have approval.

Hebrews 13:5: *I will never leave you nor forsake you. I won't fail you nor let you down.*

1 Peter 1:18-19:
You are important and valuable. I purchased you with My blood.

Song of Songs 4:7:
My beloved; there is no flaw in you!

Jeremiah 29:11:
My plan is to prosper you and give you hope and a future.

2 Corinthians 9:8: *My grace abounds toward you and you have more than enough to give to every good work.*

kindness

security

confidence

self-control

humility

I am who
Jesus says I am

faith

peace

joy

love

patience

goodness

compassion

TRUTH PRODUCES POSITIVE EMOTIONS

faith	peace
confidence	joy
security	compassion
kindness	love
humility	self-control
patience	goodness

Jesus speaks His truth and promises to all of us. Have you ever wondered why some people simply receive the truth in their hearts and experience freedom, while others hear the same truth and continue to stay in bondage to the enemy's lies? From an early age, the enemy begins to throw his fiery darts (lies) at our hearts. When we accept his lies as truth, the darts begin to penetrate our hearts and create brokenness.

THE LIE	YOUR AGREEMENT	BROKENNESS
You can't do it	I can't do it	discouragement
You're not good enough	I'm not good enough	condemnation
You're a failure	I'm a failure	shame
You're not as good as they are	I'm not as good as they are	jealousy
You lack in some way	I lack in some way	insecurity
You can't trust God	I can't really trust God	fear

This brokenness continues all our lives. Only the truth can set us free. My own heart was filled with brokenness and insecurity for many years because I believed the lies of my enemy. Because I agreed with the enemy of my soul, a negative picture was painted on the canvas of my heart, which said, *I'm not good enough. Something is wrong with me. I'm not as good as her. I lack in some way. They don't like me. I'm not as important as them. I don't qualify.* This was the picture that I had of myself. So anytime I heard the truth such as *Connie, you're wonderful. You're beautiful. You're special. You're loved,* it just leaked right out of the holes in my heart. I couldn't receive it because my heart told me that it wasn't true for me. I had already decided in my heart that I didn't qualify.

LIES PRODUCE STRONGHOLDS

A *stronghold* is a lie of the devil that you have accepted as truth. A stronghold was created in my heart because I had agreed with the lies of the devil and those lies became what I believed was true about myself. The truth couldn't take root and produce God's promises in my life because I agreed with my enemy. Jesus taught this truth in Mark 4:1-20 in the parable of the sower. He taught that you can hear the Good News about what Jesus has done for you, but the enemy immediately comes and says, *that's not true for you,* and steals the truth from your heart, so it doesn't produce fruit.

You can hear the truth your whole life, but if you don't let go of the lies and begin to agree with the truth it will never heal your brokenness and make you whole. I came to a place in my life where the pain in my heart was so great I was willing to do anything to be free. One day, in desperation, I cried out to Jesus to, "Show me the truth that will set me free." In answer to my prayer, the Holy Spirit began to show me who I am in Jesus and told me that if I would just surrender my own opinion of myself and agree with His opinion of me, my heart would be made whole, and my life would be transformed. The choice was mine: but who was I going to believe? Who was I going to devote my heart to? And who was I going to agree with: the devil and his lies or Jesus and the truth? With the Holy Spirit's help, I made a decision that day to agree with the One Who loves me. When I did, a new picture of me began to be painted on the canvas of my heart. Today it looks like this: "I am loved, abundantly blessed, favored, protected, righteous, and free, because of Jesus!"

I'd love to tell you that I only had to do that once and it took care of everything, but the truth is, the lies still come and the devil still aims his fiery darts at my heart. Every day I have to make a choice between life and death. When I hear the lies of the devil and my heart feels the symptoms of those lies, I guard my heart by turning to Jesus and asking for strength to believe Him instead of the lie. I run to the throne of grace and agree with what Jesus says about me. A lie is only a temptation until you agree with it. When you put up the shield of faith by agreeing with the One Who loves you, the lie dissipates in the light of His love.

As long as you live you will continue to hear the lies, but as you continue to turn to Jesus your heart will say more and more, "No, that is not what is true about me. I am who

God says I am because of Jesus." Jesus is your stronghold against the lies of the enemy. As you agree with the One Who loves you, your heart is made whole.

THE TRUTH	YOUR AGREEMENT	WHOLENESS
You can do it	I can do all things through Jesus	encouragement
You are very good	I am righteous in Jesus	peace
You're a success	I'm a success	joy
You're loved	I am loved	security
You are complete	I am complete in Christ	confidence
God is faithful	I can trust God completely	faith

Devote your heart to Jesus. Remember, whoever you choose to agree with is the one whose plan will come to pass in your life. Ephesians 3:20 says that God is able to bring His plan to pass in your life and do superabundantly far over and above your highest prayers, desires, thoughts, hopes or dreams when you begin to agree with the One Who loves you.

Look at the heart on page 54 and take a moment to agree with the One Who loves you. Establish your heart in His love.

PART 3

AN OAK OF RIGHTEOUSNESS

[17]I pray that Christ will be more and more at home in your hearts as you trust in him. May your roots go down deep into the soil of God's marvelous love. [18]And may you have the power to understand, as all God's people should, how wide, how long, how high, and how deep his love really is. [19]May you experience the love of Christ, though it is so great you will never fully understand it. Then you will be filled with the fullness of life and power that comes from God! [20]Now glory be to God! By His mighty power at work within us, he is able to accomplish infinitely more than we would ever dare to ask or hope.

EPHESIANS 3:17-20 NLT[1]

Chapter 7

THE GREATEST GIFT OF LOVE

¹The Spirit of God, the Master, is on me because God
anointed me. He sent me to preach good news to the poor,
heal the heartbroken, announce freedom to all captives,
pardon all prisoners. ²God sent me to announce the year
of his grace — a celebration of God's destruction of our
enemies — and to comfort all who mourn, ³to care for
the needs of all who mourn in Zion, give them bouquets
of roses instead of ashes, messages of joy instead of news
of doom, a praising heart instead of a languid spirit.
Rename them "Oaks of Righteousness"
planted by God to display his glory.

ISAIAH 61:1-3 MSG

These verses reveal that Jesus came to heal all the broken places of your heart with the Good News of His love. He came to proclaim your freedom from sin and set you free from the lies of the devil that have held you in bondage. He came to tell you of a New Covenant of Grace and to celebrate the defeat of your enemy. He came to comfort you when you're sad and meet every need of your heart. He has done all of this by making you an **oak of righteousness**.

THE MESSAGE OF GOOD NEWS IS THE GIFT OF RIGHTEOUSNESS

2 Corinthians 5:17-21:

¹⁷Anyone who belongs to Christ has become a new
person. The old life is gone; a new life has begun!

¹⁸And all of this is a gift from God, who brought us back to himself through Christ. And God has given us this task of reconciling people to him. ¹⁹For God was in Christ, reconciling the world to himself, no longer counting people's sins against them. And he gave us this wonderful message of reconciliation. ²⁰So we are Christ's ambassadors; God is making his appeal through us. We speak for Christ when we plead, "Come back to God!" ²¹For God made Christ, who never sinned, to be the offering for our sin, so that we could be made right with God through Christ. NLT

2 Corinthians 5:21:

*²¹ For He made Him who knew no sin to be sin for us, that we might become **the righteousness of God in Him.*** NKJV

The message of Good News that Jesus was sent to tell us about in Isaiah 61:1-3 is revealed again in these verses. If you belong to Jesus, you have become a brand new person. You have been given a new identity. He sent others to tell you this wonderful Good News as well. He no longer counts your sins against you. By His one sacrifice, He became sin so that you and I could be made the righteousness of God in Christ. Being declared righteous in Him is His gift of love to you and to everyone who will receive it.

THE GREATEST DEMONSTRATION OF
UNCONDITIONAL LOVE:
JESUS PAID A GREAT PRICE TO GIVE YOU THE
GIFT OF RIGHTEOUSNESS

Isaiah 53:3-11:

³He was despised and rejected — a man of sorrows, acquainted with deepest grief. We turned our backs on him and looked the other way. He was despised, and we did not care.

⁴Yet it was our weaknesses he carried; it was our sorrows that weighed him down. And we thought his troubles were a punishment from God, a punishment for his own sins! ⁵But he was pierced for our rebellion, crushed for our sins. He was beaten so we could be whole. He was whipped so we could be healed. ⁶All of us, like sheep, have strayed away. We have left God's paths to follow our own. Yet the Lord laid on him the sins of us all.

⁷He was oppressed and treated harshly, yet he never said a word. He was led like a lamb to the slaughter. And as a sheep is silent before the shearers, he did not open his mouth. ⁸Unjustly condemned, he was led away. No one cared that he died without descendants, that his life was cut short in midstream. But he was struck down for the rebellion of my people. ⁹He had done no wrong and had never deceived anyone. But he was buried like a criminal; he was put in a rich man's grave.

¹⁰But it was the LORD's good plan to crush him and cause him grief. Yet when his life is made an offering for sin, he will have many descendants. He will enjoy a long life, and the LORD's good plan will prosper in his hands. ¹¹When he sees all that is accomplished *by his anguish, he will be satisfied. And because of his experience, **my righteous servant will make it possible for many to be counted righteous**, for he will bear all their sins.* NLT

Do you really understand what Jesus did on the cross for you? You and I were sinners. We failed to meet God's requirements for righteousness. The Old Covenant stated that we had to obey all of God's laws in order to be made righteous and worthy of God's promised blessings (Deuteronomy 6:25; 28:1-66), but we all failed and were declared sinners. According to the law, we deserve punishment for our sins and we are under the curse. But Jesus loves us so much that He came to take our place. He was beaten so that you could be made whole; He was whipped in order that you might be healed. By His sacrifice, He rescued you from the curse of the law and gave you the gift of righteousness (Galatians 3:13,14). He made you and me worthy of every promised blessing of God, and we receive it simply by receiving His gift of love.

Romans 5:5-9:

⁵Such hope never disappoints or deludes or shames us, for God's love has been poured out in our hearts through the Holy Spirit Who has been given to us. ⁶While we were yet in weakness [powerless to help ourselves], at the fitting time Christ died for (in behalf of) the ungodly. ⁷Now it is an extraordinary thing for one to give his life even for an upright man, though perhaps for a noble and lovable and generous benefactor someone might even dare to die. ⁸But God shows and clearly proves His [own] love for us by

the fact that while we were still sinners, Christ (the
Messiah, the Anointed One) died for us. [9]Therefore...
*we are now justified (acquitted, **made righteous**, and*
brought into right relationship with God) by Christ's
blood. AMP

What does it mean to be made righteous? *Righteous*
means: "justified, acquitted, free from blame or guilt, holy,
innocent." *(Strong's 1342, 1343, 1344)* In being made righteous, you
are justified. In order to get a clearer understanding of this
amazing gift, let's look at the definition of *justification*:

> *It is the judicial act of God, by which he pardons*
> *all the sins of those who believe in Christ, and*
> *accounts, accepts, and **treats them as righteous** in*
> *the eye of the law. In addition to the pardon of sin,*
> *justification declares that all the claims of the law are*
> *satisfied. The law is not relaxed or set aside, but is*
> *declared to be fulfilled in the strictest sense; and so*
> ***the person justified is declared to be entitled to all***
> ***the advantages and rewards arising from perfect***
> ***obedience to the law** (Romans 5:1-10). It proceeds*
> *on the crediting to the believer by God himself of*
> *the perfect righteousness, of Jesus Christ (Romans*
> *10:3-9). Justification is not the forgiveness of a man*
> *without righteousness, but a declaration that he*
> *possesses a righteousness which perfectly and forever*
> *satisfies the law, namely, Christ's righteousness*
> *(2 Corinthians 5:21; Romans 4:6-8).[1]*

Do you see why righteousness is the greatest gift of
love? Even though you and I do not deserve to be declared

[1]Reference: http://www.christiananswers.net/dictionary/justification.html: Bible Encyclopedia

righteous because we fail at times, Jesus has given us His perfect righteousness. When God looks at you in Christ, He sees you as perfect, holy, innocent, and blameless because your sins have been forgiven and forgotten (Hebrews 8:12). God Himself declares you and me entitled to all the blessings and rewards of one who has perfectly obeyed the law even though we are guilty of many sins. It is finished! All you and I need to do is receive His gift of love.

Romans 5:16-17:

> *16Again, **the gift of God** is not like the result of the one man's sin: The judgment followed one sin and brought condemnation, but **the gift** followed many trespasses and brought justification. 17For if, by the trespass of the one man, death reigned through that one man, how much more will those who receive God's abundant provision of grace and of **the gift of righteousness** reign in life through the one man, Jesus Christ. NIV*

One man's sin brought judgment and condemnation to everyone because everyone sinned, but the gift of God is righteousness through Jesus to everyone who will receive it. If you have accepted Jesus as your Savior, you're a new person. Be conscious every day that you are the righteousness of God in Christ. It's your new identity in Jesus. You no longer have to try to be righteous. It is a gift you must only receive. This gift gives you the very nature of Jesus and qualifies you for every promised blessing of God. Every one of God's promises are "yes and amen" in your life because you are the righteousness of God in Christ Jesus! (2 Corinthians 1:20)

Remember, you learned previously that every lie the devil

throws at you is an attempt to deceive you into believing this one lie: *You're not who God says you are.*

The truth is you only need to believe one promise to qualify for every promised blessing of God:

I am the righteousness of God in Christ Jesus!

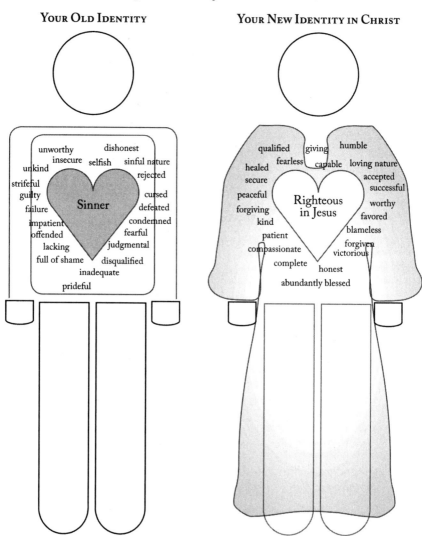

WHO ARE YOU?

What does your heart truly believe? Look back at the list of the characteristics of a sinner. The devil will try to convince you that you are still a sinner because of your failures. He wants you to believe the lie that *you are not who God says you are.* If you believe this lie, your life will produce the characteristics of a sinner, even though you truly are the righteousness of God in Christ Jesus. The belief of your heart will determine the fruit of your life.

Now look at the characteristics of the righteous. Jesus wants you to believe the truth that you are the righteousness of God in Christ. How does it make your heart feel to realize that these characteristics describe who you truly are in Jesus?

Jesus gave His name and everything He possesses to you as a gift. He took off your filthy sin-stained clothes and dressed you in a robe of righteousness. He clothed you with who He is. When He dressed you in His righteousness, He clothed you with approval, favor, forgiveness, abundant blessings, prosperity, health, kindness, love, success, and wholeness. Your Savior loves you so much that He did for you what you could never do for yourself. He gave you what you needed to qualify for every promise of God by giving you His perfect righteousness as a gift of His love. When you understand the magnitude of what Jesus accomplished for you in His finished work on the cross, you'll experience perfect peace in your heart in every situation. You'll rejoice in the truth that you are loved!

Isaiah 61:10:

¹⁰I will sing for joy in God, explode in praise from

deep in my soul! He dressed me up in a suit of salvation, he outfitted me in a robe of righteousness, as a bridegroom who puts on a tuxedo and a bride a jeweled tiara. MSG

So rejoice in the One Who finished the work for you. You are dressed in a robe of righteousness and you have everything you need in Jesus. The next time you face a challenge and the devil attempts to deceive you with his lies, remember who you are. You can quench all his fiery darts, by rejoicing in this one truth and declaring, **"I am the righteousness of God in Christ Jesus!"** You are an oak of righteousness and as you agree with the One Who loves you, you'll see your life display the glory of God.

Chapter 8

THE RIGHTEOUS SHALL LIVE
BY FAITH

[17] This Good News tells us how God makes us right in his
sight. This is accomplished from start to finish by faith.
As the Scriptures say, "It is through faith
that a righteous person has life."
ROMANS 1:17 NLT[2]

The Gospel is Good News. It is the message of God proving His amazing love for you and me by making us righteous in His sight through Jesus. This is accomplished from start to finish by faith.

You learned previously that the word faith comes from the Greek word *pistis* (Strong's 4102) which means:

- ⚜ reliance upon Jesus for salvation
- ⚜ to trust or believe
- ⚜ to agree with God

The Bible tells us that the righteous shall live by faith.

2 Corinthians 4:13:

[13] It is written: "I believed, therefore, I have
spoken." With that same spirit of faith we also
believe and therefore speak. NIV

Jesus made you an oak of righteousness. As your heart begins to really believe this truth, you'll confidently speak

His promises over yourself and your family. Your roots will go down deep into the soil of God's marvelous love as you agree with the One Who loves you.

Ephesians 3:17:

> *[17]I pray that Christ will be more and more at home in your hearts as you trust in him. May your roots go down deep into the soil of God's marvelous love. NLT[1]*

RIGHTEOUSNESS IS A FREE GIFT

For quite a few years of my Christian life I wasn't living loved because I was trying to earn something that had already been given to me as a gift. I mistakenly thought that I had to do something else besides receive God's gracious gift to be made righteous and worthy of God's approval and blessing. Unconsciously my heart believed that what Jesus did on the cross for me wasn't good enough, and I had to complete His work by adding something to it. Deep down in my heart I believed this lie of the enemy and it kept me in bondage for many years.

Thank goodness I was set free when the Holy Spirit began to reveal to me the Good News that you and I are already righteous because of Jesus. There is not one thing that we can add to what Jesus did on the cross to make us any more righteous then we are right now. There are no, "Five Steps to Answered Prayer," or "Four Steps to Pleasing God," "Three Steps to Prosperity," or even "Two Steps to Healing"! There is only one step and it's faith in Jesus, and when we trust in Him, we become righteous.

That is the only thing necessary to qualify us for all the promises God has made to the righteous. They are our inheritance in Christ because of His great gift of love. He purchased them for us with His blood so that you and I could have peace in this world.

PROMISES GOD HAS MADE TO THE RIGHTEOUS

PROSPERITY Proverbs 13:21: *Prosperity is the reward of the righteous. NIV*

BLESSING AND FAVOR Psalm 5:12: *For surely, O LORD, you bless the righteous; you surround them with your favor as with a shield. NIV* (Also see, **Deuteronomy 28:1-13**)

FINANCIAL ABUNDANCE Psalm 37:17,19: *The LORD sustains the righteous. 19They will not be ashamed in the time of evil, and in the days of famine they will have abundance. NASB*

BLESSED TO BE A BLESSING 2 Corinthians 9:8-11: *8God is able to make all grace abound to you, so that in all things at all times, having all that you need, you will abound in every good work. 9As it is written: "He has scattered abroad his gifts to the poor; his righteousness endures forever." 10Now he who supplies seed to the sower and bread for food will also supply and increase your store of seed and will enlarge the harvest of your righteousness. 11You will be made rich in every way so that you can be generous on every occasion. NIV*

DELIVERANCE Psalm 34:15,17,19: *15The eyes of the LORD are on the righteous and his ears are attentive to their cry; 17The righteous cry out, and the LORD hears them; he delivers them from all their troubles. 19A righteous man may* *have many troubles, but the LORD delivers him from them all.* NIV

A BLESSED FAMILY Proverbs 3:33: *The Lord . . . declares . . . blessed (joyful and favored with blessings) the home of the just and consistently righteous.* AMP

SAVED AND DELIVERED CHILDREN Proverbs 11:21: *[The] seed of the righteous shall be delivered.* KJV (Also see, Isaiah 59:21)

DESIRES GRANTED Proverbs 10:24: *The desire of the righteous shall be granted.* KJV

POWERFUL AND EFFECTIVE PRAYERS James 5:16: *The prayer of a righteous man is powerful and effective.* NIV (Also see, 1 John 5:14-16)

PROTECTION Proverbs 12:21: *No [actual] evil, misfortune, or calamity shall come upon the righteous.* AMP (Also see, Psalm 91)

Wow! What wonderful promises Jesus has purchased for you and me. Does your heart really believe these promises are true for you? Do you really believe that you are the righteousness of God in Christ? How does your heart respond when you read these verses? Are you thankful for what Jesus made available to you? Or does your heart question God's love and promises? Remember, the righteous shall have true life by agreeing with the One Who loves them!

Just last year the economy began to decline and the news media was giving all kinds of bad reports about the financial state of our country. People were losing their jobs and there was fear in the hearts of many people. I remember very distinctly turning my heart to the Lord and asking, "Father, what do You say about this bad economy?" What do you say about the righteous?"

The Holy Spirit reminded me of Psalm 37:17-19 which says that the Lord will take care of the righteous and in the time of famine they will have abundance. Peace came over my heart as I thought upon this promise that Jesus had purchased for me. I heard the Lord say to me, "Because many of my people don't see themselves as truly righteous in me and won't believe what I say about them, they won't experience the abundance that I have provided for them through Jesus. But those who do believe will experience peace and abundance during this time of famine." I responded by saying, "Oh, thank You Jesus, for making me righteous. Thank You for loving me so much and giving me the grace to trust You! Thank You for your promise to take care of us during these bad economic times by blessing us with abundance. Your promise is an anchor for my soul. You are my peace and I love you, Lord."

Shortly after this conversation with Jesus, I was sitting on the back porch of my home with my entire family. My daughter-in-law began talking with us about how the economy was affecting the company she worked for and how many of the people she worked with were being laid off. I encouraged her by reminding her that she is the righteousness of God in Christ and that she has the favor and blessing of God because of Jesus. Even if she did get laid off, God would provide her with a better job. We had nothing to worry about because God's promise to the righteous during hard economic times is that we will have an abundance.

Now, I haven't always responded in this way to God's promises to the righteous. Many years ago — when I didn't understand the amazing love God showed toward me by making me righteous in Jesus — the fruit of my life was fear and insecurity. Even though I had read this verse many times, my heart was unsure that God would really take care of me. I questioned God's promise instead of receiving it. I wasn't living loved by Him by agreeing with what He said about me. But even though I was experiencing fear and lack instead of abundance, it still didn't make the promise any less true.

Today, I guard my heart from the lies of the devil by thinking daily upon the truth that Jesus has made me righteous. My heart has become convinced of His great love for me, so I don't allow the devil to deceive me any more by questioning God's promise of who I am in Jesus.

Recently, I had another opportunity to express what I believe to my family. I boldly shared with them that we are the righteousness of God in Christ Jesus and if God says we will experience abundance during the time of famine then that is exactly what is true for us. I told them that we don't look to the right or to the left and question God's promise because of what is happening around us. We keep our eyes on Jesus and agree with the One Who loves us. We choose to trust Him and speak His word over our lives because we are righteous in Jesus. *This is what it means to live by faith.* My family all agreed that we are blessed because of Jesus!

True to His word and promise, God blessed my husband's business and it grew by twenty-five percent; my son and daughter-in-law were both promoted in their jobs, and we experienced abundance during this time of "famine" because we are the righteousness of God in Christ Jesus and we believe it! Woo hoo!

Take time right now to read back over the promises that God has made to the righteous. Insert your name in each verse and let His promises to you penetrate deep within your heart. As you do this thank Jesus for each one.

Let your roots go down deep into the soil of God's marvelous love by thankfully acknowledging these promises to be true for you and your family. You are qualified because you are the righteousness of God in Christ Jesus! Remember: **the righteous shall live by faith.** You can experience peace in every single situation by agreeing with the One Who loves you, and you can live free from fear and insecurity as you live loved by Him.

Chapter 9

A HEART ESTABLISHED
IN RIGHTEOUSNESS

14You shall establish yourself in righteousness....: you shall be far from even the thought of oppression or destruction, for you shall not fear, and from terror, for it will not come near you.

ISAIAH 54:14 AMP

You've previously learned that the devil's main objective is to deceive you into believing that you're not who God says you are. His lies are intended to oppress you and cause you to experience fear in your heart. In contrast, when your heart is established in righteousness Isaiah 54:14 above says that *the thought of oppression will be far from you.* You may be tempted with a negative thought, but your heart will say, *No, that's not who I am. I am the righteousness of God in Christ Jesus, and His promises are true in my life.* Fear won't be able to take root in your heart when you know and believe who you are in Jesus.

HOW DO YOU BECOME ESTABLISHED IN RIGHTEOUSNESS?

Ephesians 4:23-24:

> *23Instead, **let the Spirit renew your thoughts and attitudes.** 24Put on your new nature, created to be like God—truly righteous and holy.* NLT²

This verse shows you the importance of being constantly renewed in the spirit of your mind. By inviting Jesus into your thought processes and letting the Holy Spirit change the way you think, you will be strengthened in your faith as your heart becomes established in righteousness. The enemy is constantly trying to oppress us by filling our minds with his lies. If we allow ourselves to believe them, we'll live in bondage and darkness.

Just the other day a negative thought came into my mind about a particular person in my life. Thankfully, I immediately recognized the thought as not being a part of who I am because I know that I am the righteousness of God in Christ Jesus, and I have the mind of Christ (1 Corinthians 2:16). Even knowing that, I still invited Jesus into my thought process."Lord," I said, "help me to see this person through your eyes and from your perspective." The Holy Spirit was faithful to once again establish my heart in righteousness. He empowered me to see the best in this person, and the thought of oppression stayed far away from me.

In another recent experience, my husband came to me with some bad news about his business. As he talked about the situation, I immediately turned my thoughts to Jesus and invited Him into my thought process, *Lord, I thank You that You are our Provider. You abundantly supply all of our needs. Thank You for making us righteous and surrounding us with favor as a shield. I trust You, Lord.* I was then able to tell my husband, "God will work it out for our good. We are blessed because of Jesus!" Fear didn't even have a chance to take root in my heart because my heart was established in righteousness and the thought of oppression stayed far from me.

Isaiah 32:17-18:

> *17The fruit of righteousness will be peace; the effect of righteousness will be quietness and confidence forever. 18My people will live in peaceful dwelling places, in secure homes, in undisturbed places of rest.* NIV

When your heart is established in righteousness, the fruit of your life is peace and confidence forever! Your home is filled with peace and security. Your heart is undisturbed as you rest in the truth that you are loved!

Psalm 112:6-8:

> *6...a righteous man will be remembered forever. 7He will have no fear of bad news; his heart is steadfast, trusting in the LORD. 8His heart is secure, he will have no fear; in the end he will look in triumph on his foes.* NIV

The above scripture describes the kind of life that Jesus died for you to live. He wants your heart to be established in righteousness, free from fear, and secure in His love. He wants you to have no fear of bad news because you know who you are and the promise you have in Him. When bad news comes, your first response is to agree with the One Who loves you! You are victorious in every situation because you are the righteousness of God in Christ Jesus!

HOW A HEART ESTABLISHED IN RIGHTEOUSNESS RESPONDS TO BAD NEWS

Bad news: *The economy is bad and people are losing their jobs.*
A heart established in righteousness responds by saying:
"I am the righteousness of God in Christ Jesus! I prosper during famine. Thank you, Jesus, for taking care of me." (Psalm 37: 15-19)

Bad news: *The weather is looking bad. A tornado may come near the area where you live.*
A heart established in righteousness responds by saying:
"I am righteous in Jesus. No evil or calamity comes near my home. Thank You, Lord, for protecting me and my family." (Proverbs 12:21; Psalm 91)

Bad news: *People are saying evil things about you.*
A heart established in righteousness responds by saying:
"I am the righteousness of God in Christ Jesus! My righteousness shines like the noon day sun. Thank You, Jesus, that what You say about me is true. You think I'm wonderful!" (Psalm 37:6; Psalm 139:14-18)

Bad news: *Your spouse is in a bad mood and is upset with you again.*
A heart established in righteousness responds by saying:
"I am righteous in Jesus and my home is joyful and favored with blessings. Thank You, Lord, that You surround me with favor as a shield." (Psalm 5:12)

Bad news: *You are experiencing symptoms of sickness in your body.*

A heart established in righteousness responds by saying: "I am the righteousness of God in Christ Jesus! I walk in divine health! Thank you, Lord, for forgiving all my sins and healing all my diseases." (Psalm 103:2-3)

Bad news: *Your children are making poor choices.*

A heart established in righteousness responds by saying: "I am righteous in Jesus! My prayers for my children are powerful and effective. Lord, I can be very sure that You'll rescue my children (Proverbs 11:21). Thank You for working in their hearts and giving them the desire and power to do what pleases You." (Philippians 2:13).

Psalm 1:1-3:

> *¹Blessed (happy, fortunate, prosperous, and enviable) is the man whose... ²delight and desire are in the law of the Lord, and on His law (the precepts, the instructions, the teachings of God) he habitually meditates (ponders and studies) by day and by night. ³And he shall be like a tree firmly planted [and tended] by the streams of water, ready to bring forth its fruit in its season; its leaf also shall not fade or wither; and everything he does shall prosper." AMP*

JESUS MADE YOU AN OAK OF RIGHTEOUSNESS, PLANTED BY GOD TO DISPLAY HIS GLORY

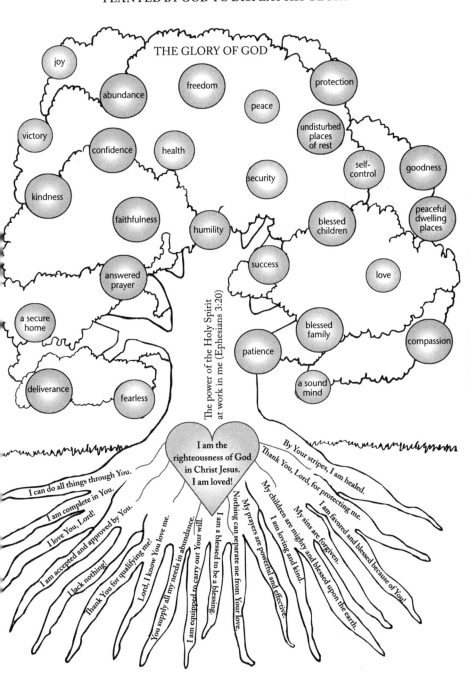

The tree on page 81 illustrates the power of the Holy Spirit at work in you. (Ephesians 3:20)

Ephesians 3:17:

> [17]*I pray that Christ will be more and more at home in your hearts as you trust in him. May your roots go down deep into the soil of God's marvelous love. NLT*[1]

This tree is a picture of who you are in Jesus and the kind of life that He came to give you. Invite Jesus into your thought processes daily by thinking upon the truth of who you are in Him. Let Him change the way you think about yourself and establish your heart in righteousness. As you do this, you'll be like a tree planted by streams of living water, and your roots will go down deep into the soil of God's marvelous love. Watch as the Holy Spirit brings out the fruit of righteousness in your life as you agree with the One Who loves you.

Remember: When your heart is established in righteousness the thought of oppression is far from you. You will not fear because you are secure in God's love!

PART 4

LIVING SECURELY IN THE FATHER'S LOVE

[17]May Christ through your faith [actually] dwell (settle down, abide, make His permanent home) in your hearts! May you be rooted deep in love and founded securely on love, [18]that you may have the power and be strong to apprehend and grasp with all the saints [God's devoted people, the experience of that love] what is the breadth and length and height and depth [of it]; [19][that you may really come] to know [practically, through experience for yourselves] the love of Christ, which far surpasses mere knowledge [without experience]; that you may be filled [through all your being] unto all the fullness of God [may have the richest measure of the divine Presence, and become a body wholly filled and flooded with God Himself]!

[20]Now to Him Who, by (in consequence of) the [action of His] power that is at work within us, is able to [carry out His purpose and] do superabundantly, far over and above all that we [dare] ask or think [infinitely beyond our highest prayers, desires, thoughts, hopes, or dreams] — [21]To Him be glory in the church and in Christ Jesus throughout all generations forever and ever.
Amen (so be it).

EPHESIANS 3:17-21 AMP

Chapter 10

LIVING SECURELY IN THE FATHER'S LOVE

17May Christ through your faith [actually] dwell…in your hearts! May you be rooted deep in love and founded securely on love.

EPHESIANS 3:17 AMP

In Ephesians 3:17 above the Apostle Paul, inspired by the Holy Spirit, prayed that you would live securely in your Heavenly Father's love. You are a child of the King and it delights His heart when you live loved by Him. The fullness of life Jesus came to give you is found in realizing how dearly you are loved by your Heavenly Father and allowing His words of love to change the beliefs of your heart.

WHAT DOES IT MEAN TO LIVE SECURELY IN THE FATHER'S LOVE?

Secure: "assured of one's good opinion of you; confident; free from fear or worry"

Insecure: "not sure of one's good opinion of you; not confident; beset by worry or fear"

Every day we are faced with opportunities to be insecure. Have you ever been concerned about someone's opinion of you? Have you feared being rejected? Has someone's negative attitude toward you ever caused your heart to feel anxious? I have experienced every one of these symptoms of insecurity. But I have also experienced the freedom that comes from knowing who I am in Jesus and realizing that the only opinion of me that truly matters is my Heavenly Father's opinion. His perfect love sets me free from insecurity (1 John 4:18).

If your value comes from other people's opinions of you and whether or not they accept or approve of you, you'll always be insecure because their opinion can change from day to day. On the other hand, your Heavenly Father's good opinion of you never changes because you are in Christ. Jesus gave you His perfect righteousness, and you are just like Him in this world (1 John 4:17).

Ephesians 1:5-6:
> *5For He foreordained us, (destined us, planned in love for us) to be adopted... as His own children through Jesus Christ, in accordance with the purpose of His will, [because it pleased Him and was His kind intent].* AMP

> *6...to the praise of the glory of His grace, by which* **He made us accepted in the beloved.** NKJV

Accepted: "to endue with special honor; to be highly favored; to be well pleased"

When you put your faith in Jesus, you became one with Him. It pleased the Father to make you His son or daughter through Jesus. In His perfect love, He made you fully accepted in the beloved!

In John 17:23, when Jesus prayed for us, He said, *"Father, You love them, as much as You love me".* NLT[1] This means that your Heavenly Father feels toward you the exact same way He feels toward Jesus!

Matthew 3:16-17:

> ¹⁶*After his baptism, as Jesus came up out of the water, the heavens were opened and he saw the Spirit of God descending like a dove and settling on him. ¹⁷And a voice from heaven said, "This is my beloved Son, and I am fully pleased with him."* NLT¹

Because you are in the beloved, the Father is saying the same thing about you. You are His beloved son or daughter and He is fully pleased with you because of your faith in Jesus.

Shortly after Jesus received His Father's complete approval and heard Him say, "You are My beloved Son," the devil came to tempt Him with the same lie he uses on all of us, *You're not who God says you are.* He questioned Jesus' identity. In **Matthew 4:3** the devil said, *"If you are the Son of God, change these stones into loaves of bread."* NLT¹

In Matthew 4:4, Jesus resisted the devil by saying, *"No! The Scriptures say, 'People need more than bread for their life; they must feed on every word of God.'"* (NLT¹)

In other words, Jesus was saying, "My identity comes only from my Father's opinion of me. I choose to feed on every word He says about me. I am who my Father says I am!"

Not only did the devil challenge Jesus' identity, it was constantly being called into question by the people around Him. In spite of the fact that Jesus was continually being judged negatively, His heart was secure in His Father's perfect love. Jesus didn't seek man's approval or worry about their opinion of Him because He lived loved by His Father.

JESUS IS OUR EXAMPLE OF WHAT IT LOOKS LIKE TO TRULY LIVE LOVED

Read what Jesus said in John 5:30-32, 37, 41-42:

> *30 "But I do nothing without consulting the Father. I judge as I am told.... 31 If I were to testify on my own behalf, my testimony would not be valid. 32 But someone else is also testifying about me, and I can assure you that everything he says about me is true. 37 "And the Father himself has also testified about me.... 41 "Your approval or disapproval means nothing to me, 42 because I know you don't have God's love within you." NLT[1]*

Jesus lived free from insecurity because He only let what the Father said about Him enter into His heart. Verse 30 reveals that He did nothing without consulting His Father. He asked, listened, and responded to every word He heard His Father say. He was so secure in His Father's love that man's approval or disapproval meant nothing to Him. All He focused on was what His Father said about Him, and He was convinced that everything His Father said was true. He lived free from the fear of what others thought of Him because He was secure in His Father's approval. What His Father said about Him was all that mattered.

In John 5:44 Jesus said:

> *44 How is it possible for you to believe [how can you*

> *learn to believe], you who [are content to seek and]*
> *receive praise and honor and glory from one another,*
> *and yet do not seek the praise and honor and glory*
> *which come from Him Who alone is God? AMP*

Jesus was saying that if you value other people's opinion of you more than God's, you will never truly believe and trust Him. You'll live in insecurity your whole life if man's approval and acceptance is more important to you than God's.

John 8:14-15, 25-26, 54, 55:

> *[14]Jesus told them, "These claims are valid even*
> *though I make them about myself. For I know*
> *where I came from and where I am going, but you*
> *don't know this about me. [15]You judge me with all*
> *your human limitations...." [25]"Tell us who you are,"*
> *they demanded. Jesus replied, "I am the one I have*
> *always claimed to be. [26]...I say only what I have*
> *heard from [my Father] and he is true. [54]If I am*
> *merely boasting about myself, it doesn't count. But*
> *it is my Father who says these glorious things about*
> *me.... [55]If I said otherwise I would be as great a*
> *liar as you!" NLT[1]*

What a powerful way to live! Here we see a wonderful example of what it means to live securely in the Father's love. Jesus showed us what it looks like to truly live loved. He knew the glorious things the Father said about Him were true, and He only said what He heard His Father say. Jesus agreed with the One Who loved Him. He realized that any opinion that wasn't in agreement with His Father was a lie. He knew that if He said anything about Himself other than what His Father said He would be as great a liar as the men who were judging Him falsely.

I SAY ONLY WHAT I HEAR MY FATHER SAY

Take a moment to listen to the glorious things your Heavenly Father says about you in Christ:

My beloved,
You are the apple of My eye, the delight of My heart, and I am fully pleased with you! My plans are to prosper you and give you a hope and a future. I've equipped you with everything you need to carry out My will. You are forgiven, righteous, capable, anointed, abundantly blessed, highly favored, qualified, complete, valuable, important, and free from all sin. You have the mind of Christ. I fully accept you and approve of you completely. Nothing can ever separate you from My love.
Your Heavenly Father

When you live securely in the Father's love, man's approval or disapproval means nothing to you; you value God's opinion over the opinion of any man. You know who you are in Jesus, and you say only what you hear your Heavenly Father saying about you. If you were simply boasting about yourself, it would count for nothing, but these are the glorious things your Heavenly Father says about you in Christ, and what He says is true. Any other opinion is a lie.

The next time the devil tempts you to question your identity in Christ, follow Jesus' example. Resist the devil's lies by saying, "I live by every word my Heavenly Father says about me. I am who my Father says I am because of Jesus!"

Chapter 11

THE PARABLE OF THE FATHER'S LOVE

[8] "...with everlasting love I will have compassion on you,"
says the Lord, your Redeemer. [9] "Just as I swore in the time
of Noah that I would never again let a flood cover the
earth, so now I swear that I will never again be angry
and punish you. [10] For the mountains may move and the
hills disappear, but even then my faithful love for you will
remain. My covenant of blessing will never be broken,"
says the Lord, who has mercy on you.

ISAIAH 54:8-10 NLT [2]

As I've taken this journey of learning to live loved by my Heavenly Father, one understanding that has brought much peace to my heart is the truth that even when I fail, my Heavenly Father's opinion of me never changes. No matter how I may fall short, I can always run to Him to receive His love and forgiveness because He is never angry at me. Instead, He patiently waits for me to turn toward Him and establish my heart once again in His love.

Because the Old Covenant is full of stories of God pouring His wrath and anger on people because of their sin, many people have come to believe a lie which has caused them to misunderstand their Father's heart toward his wayward children. What they don't understand is that those of us who have accepted Jesus as our Savior, are no longer under God's wrath (Romans 5:8-9; John 3:17-18). Because a New Covenant has been established through Jesus, we no longer have to fear God's anger or judgment. When we fail our Heavenly Father only feels compassion toward us because of His great love.

In Isaiah 54:8-10, you can see this wonderful promise from your Heavenly Father. He says that He will never again be angry with you because of your sins. His heart will always feel love and compassion toward you. You can live securely in His love.

Hebrews 12:5-11 teaches that your Heavenly Father will correct you when you do wrong, but because of His promise to you in Isaiah 54:9, you can be completely confident that He will never be angry at you.

Any time you sin it's because you've taken on a different opinion of yourself other than the one the Father has of you and have forgotten who you are in Jesus (James 1:22-24). When you go your own way, the Father only feels compassion toward you, and He corrects your wrong opinion of yourself.

Let's take a look at a parable in the Bible often called the "Prodigal Son," which would be better titled "The Parable of the Father's Love." It is a story that clearly demonstrates our Heavenly Father's heart of love toward his wayward children. It's a beautiful picture of the unchanging, unconditional, constant love of a father for his rebellious and disobedient son. Although the son was unfaithful, the father's love for him never failed.

Luke 15:11-24:

> *[11]There was a certain man who had two sons; [12]and the younger of them said to his father, Father, give me the part of the property that falls [to me]. And he divided the estate between them.*
>
> *[13]And not many days after that, the younger son gathered up all that he had and journeyed into a distant country, and there he wasted his fortune in reckless and loose [from restraint] living. [14]And when he had spent all he had, a mighty famine came upon that country, and he began to fall behind and be in want.*
>
> *[15]So he went and forced (glued) himself upon one of the citizens of that country, who sent him into his fields to feed the hogs. [16]And he would gladly have fed on and filled his belly with the carob pods that the hogs were eating, but [they could not satisfy his hunger and] nobody gave him anything [better].*
>
> *[17]Then when he came to himself, he said, How many hired servants of my father have enough food, and [even food] to spare, but I am perishing (dying) here of hunger! [18]I will get up and go to my father, and I will say to him, Father, I have sinned against heaven and in your sight. [19]I am no longer worthy to be called your son; [just] make me like one of your hired servants.*
>
> *[20]So he got up and came to his [own] father. But while he was still a long way off, his father saw*

him and was moved with pity and tenderness [for him]; and he ran and embraced him and kissed him [fervently]. ₂₁And the son said to him, Father, I have sinned against heaven and in your sight; I am no longer worthy to be called your son... [I no longer deserve to be recognized as a son of yours]!

²²But the father said to his bond servants, "Bring quickly the best robe (the festive robe of honor) and put it on him; and give him a ring for his hand and sandals for his feet. ²³And bring out the... fattened calf and kill it; and let us revel and feast and be happy and make merry, ²⁴Because this my son was dead and is alive again; he was lost and is found! And they began to revel and feast and make merry.
AMP

In this parable, we see that the younger son took his inheritance and wasted it on a sinful lifestyle. He decided in his heart that going his own way would get him what he wanted. Just like Eve, he believed the lie that he lacked in some way and he was going to get his needs met outside of his relationship with his father.

We have all, at one time or another, been prodigal sons. We've all felt a sense of lack and looked outside of our relationship with God to meet our needs. We've all gone our own way and fallen short of the glory of God (Romans 3:12).

Sin is its own punishment. The Bible says the wages which sin pays is death (Romans 6:23 *AMP*). It wasn't the father's plan for the son to live with the pigs and be in want, but he loved his son enough to allow him the choice to either live in his love, or to take on his own opinion and choose his own way. One hundred percent of the time going our own way will bring heartache and pain into our lives. At one time or another, we've all found ourselves eating with the pigs, our hearts filled with shame, condemnation, disappointment, and discouragement because we chose to believe the lie of our enemy instead of living in our Father's love. Our Heavenly Father has compassion toward us when we sin because he knows the shame sin brings and the pain it causes our hearts.

In verses 14-16 of the parable, we see that the son's poor choices eventually led him to lack and brokenness. He found himself hungry, sad, and rejected by all his friends. He finally came to realize that even the servants of his father's house had a better life than he did. Because of his failure, the son's opinion of himself was that he was *no longer worthy to be called a son.* But even though he believed the lie that he deserved to pay for his sins, that was not how his father felt about him.

From the father's perspective, there was no condemnation, only unconditional love and compassion toward his son. He ran toward him and embraced him and kissed him fervently, which must have shocked the son. He expected his father to be angry and hard on him, making him earn his way back into his graces. But even though the father poured his love upon him, the son still believed in his heart that he was undeserving and unworthy to receive his father's blessing. The shame in his heart and the negative opinion he had of himself is revealed in these words which he spoke to his father, *"Father I have sinned against heaven and before you; I am no longer worthy to be called your son."* But what the boy expected and what happened were two very different things. The father didn't even acknowledge his son's sins! His focus was not on reprimanding him for wasting his inheritance, but rather on reminding him of who he was, and restoring him to the honored position as his son.

The father's heart towards his son is revealed in what he said to his servants:

"Quickly, bring the best robe and put it on my son." The robe was a symbol of honor. The father dressed his son with a robe of righteousness to remind him of who he is.

"Put a ring on his finger." The ring was a symbol of authority. It meant he belonged to his father and everything the father had was his.

"Put shoes on his feet." Slaves went barefoot, but sons wore shoes. This signified that he had not lost his position as his father's son.

"Kill the fatted calf." A sacrifice was made to take away his sin and shame forever.

In the ancient world there was no way of preserving meat. When guests were invited for a meal, an appropriately sized animal was killed, enough to sufficiently feed the guests. For a small family, a chicken or a pigeon would be adequate; for two families, a duck or a goose would be enough. If more people were invited, it would be appropriate to kill a goat or a lamb. The killing of a fatted calf was only done if the entire village was invited. This was indeed an event of great importance. It was a great celebration and meant that someone very special was being honored.

There was even further significance to this killing of a fatted calf. The actual slaughter of the animal would take place right at the threshold of the doorway. As each guest stepped across the blood of the slain animal, it signified that the past had been left behind. As the son himself stepped over the blood of the animal, he knew it meant that he was completely forgiven and his past mistakes were forgotten. It was a sign of his father's total and complete acceptance and forgiveness. The father welcomed him back unconditionally, his heart filled with joy as he honored his son.

Jesus used this story to give us a picture of the amazing love the Father has toward us! We've all failed at times and done things that we knew were wrong; we've all wanted to run and hide just like Adam and Eve did in the garden. Isn't it wonderful to know that when you fail, your Heavenly Father is watching and waiting for you to turn your heart toward him just like the father in this story did? He runs toward you to embrace you and fully accepts you as His beloved child. He removes your shame by reminding you of who you are in Jesus, and corrects your wrong opinion of yourself. He wants you to know that you are not defined by your sins or your past mistakes. You are defined by the truth that you are a royal son or daughter of the King and that you are extravagantly loved by Him. Knowing this, you can live securely in His love.

Zephaniah 3:17:

> [17] *The Lord your God is in the midst of you, a Mighty One, a Savior [Who saves]! He will rejoice over you with joy; He will rest [in silent satisfaction] and in His love He will be silent and make no mention [of past sins, or even recall them]; He will exult over you with singing.* AMP

Chapter 12

ARE YOU LIVING AS A SON OR A SLAVE?

In the Parable of the Father's love, there were actually two sons: the younger one whom we've read about, and an older brother who stayed behind with the father. Even though the older son didn't get lost in the world like his younger brother had, he was lost in self-righteousness, living life as a slave instead of a son. Like his younger brother, he had not yet learned to truly live loved by his father.

Luke 15:25-32:

> ^{25} *"Meanwhile, the older son was in the field. When he came near the house, he heard music and dancing.* ^{26} *So he called one of the servants and asked him what was going on.* ^{27} *'Your brother has come,' he replied, 'and your father has killed the fattened calf because he has him back safe and sound.'*
>
> ^{28} *The older brother became angry and refused to go in. So his father went out and pleaded with him.* ^{29} *But he answered his father, 'Look! All these years I've been slaving for you and never disobeyed your orders. Yet you never gave me even a young goat so I could celebrate with my friends.* ^{30} *But when this son of yours who has squandered your property with prostitutes comes home, you kill the fattened calf for him!'*

³¹ "'My son,' the father said, 'you are always with me, and everything I have is yours. ³²But we had to celebrate and be glad, because this brother of yours was dead and is alive again; he was lost and is found.'" NIV

The older son in this story was a very hard worker. He made sure to point out that while the younger son was out being rebellious and wasting his life, he remained faithful to his father. A closer look at this story reveals to us that even though this older, more responsible brother had not left home like his younger brother had, he wasn't living life as a son who enjoyed a loving relationship with his father. Rather he was living like a slave trying to earn his father's love and approval. In verse 29 this is revealed when he says, *"I've been slaving for you."* The older brother saw himself more as a faithful servant than a beloved son.

Upon the return of the disobedient younger son, the father decided to throw a great celebration and restore him to his honored position as his beloved son. The older son, hard at work in the field, heard the rejoicing, and came in to investigate. Seeing the reason for the celebration, *he became very angry.* Furious because of the blessing his younger brother received from their father, he withdrew himself from fellowship with his brother. In his mind, his brother did not deserve to have others celebrating with him because of his poor choices. His brother needed to pay for his bad behavior. Even when the father came to this older son and pleaded with him to come celebrate with the family and be restored to fellowship with his younger brother, the older son's heart was filled with *disapproval and judgment. This son's actions revealed* that he had not spent time getting to know his father because he didn't understand His father's heart of unconditional love.

THE OLDER SON WAS GUILTY OF SELF-RIGHTEOUSNESS

When the father came out to talk with his enraged older son, the son immediately called the father's attention to all the wonderful things he'd done for him over the years. In verse 29 he stated that he had never disobeyed one of his father's commands and had worked tirelessly for his father for years. This attitude sounds very similar to that of the proud Pharisee in Luke 18:9 whom Jesus described as *"certain ones who trusted in themselves that they were righteous, and viewed others with contempt."* Trusting in your good works rather than trusting in Jesus for your righteousness invariably results in a feeling of superiority over others. It causes a person's heart to be judgmental instead of compassionate toward those who have sinned.

The older brother became **jealous** of his younger brother when his father showered him with honor and blessings. In verses 29-30 he said, *29 "Look! All these years I've been slaving for you and never disobeyed your orders. Yet you never gave me even a young goat so I could celebrate with my friends. 30 But when this son of yours who has squandered your property with prostitutes comes home, you kill the fattened calf for him!"*

This hard working, faithful, devoted son, who had never committed the type of sins his younger brother had, still carried sin within his own heart. His heart was filled with anger, jealousy, self-righteousness and judgment because he was not truly living loved by his father. He didn't realize that it wasn't his hard work and devoted service that qualified him for his father's approval and blessing. Everything the father owned already belonged to him simply because he was his son.

Notice the words the father uses to correct his oldest son, *31"'My son,' the father said, 'you are always with me, and everything I have is yours. 32But we had to celebrate and be glad, because this brother of yours was dead and is alive again; he was lost and is found.'"* (Verses 31-32).

The father doesn't reprimand his older son for his anger, jealousy, judgment, or self righteousness, instead he corrects him in the same way he corrected his younger son, by simply reminding him of who he was. The father says, "You are my beloved son and everything I have belongs to you. Don't you realize how much I love you? This brother of yours was lost in his sin, but he has come back to the family. Come celebrate with us."

THE FATHER INVITED HIS ELDER SON TO LIVE IN HIS LOVE

The Father knew that if his elder boy accepted the truth about his position as his son, all the anger, jealousy, judgment and self-righteousness in his heart would disappear. The relationship between him and his brother would be restored, and his heart would rejoice in his brother's blessing. When we live securely in our Heavenly Father's unconditional love and acceptance, we are free to extend that same unconditional love and acceptance toward our brothers and sisters in Christ. Neither son was living loved because they didn't view themselves the way their father did. They both focused on their actions to determine whether or not they were worthy of their father's love. The younger son was condemned because of his failures while the older son was prideful because of his good works, and it caused brokenness in both of their hearts. Yet the father patiently waited for both of them to simply embrace their true identity and begin to live loved by Him.

I can relate to both sons in this story. There have been times in my Christian life when my failures have made me feel unworthy of God's blessings. There have also been times when I tried so hard to please God through my "good works" and "faithfulness" that I judged those whom I felt were "unfaithful" to be unworthy of God's blessings. I have felt anger, jealousy, and judgment in my heart toward my brothers and sisters in Christ because I wasn't living loved by my Heavenly Father.

Today I have learned to live securely in my Father's love and it has caused my heart to be filled with love and compassion toward those who have not fully embraced who they are in Jesus. Jesus came to set us free from the slavery of sin in all of its forms. He came so that we could live loved by the King.

Galatians 4:4-7:

> *⁴But when the right time came, God sent his Son, born of a woman, subject to the law. ⁵God sent him to buy freedom for us who were slaves to the law, so that he could adopt us as his very own children.*

> *⁶And because you Gentiles have become his children, God has sent the Spirit of his Son in your hearts, and now you can call God your dear Father. ⁷Now you are no longer a slave but God's own child. And since you are his child everything he has belongs to you." NLT[1]*

What security you can live in by simply embracing the truth that you are a son or daughter of the King and everything He has belongs to you because of Jesus. You no longer have to live as a slave trying to earn your master's approval and blessing by your "good works." You can live loved by realizing that you already have your Heavenly Father's approval and blessing simply because you are His child. When you live securely in your Heavenly Father's unconditional love, you'll live free from sin, and you'll be free to love others in the same way that He loves you.

PART 5

ABUNDANTLY FREE

[17] I pray that Christ will be more and more at home in your hearts as you trust in him. May your roots go down deep into the soil of God's marvelous love. [18] And may you have the power to understand, as all God's people should, how wide, how long, how high, and how deep his love really is. [19] May you experience the love of Christ, though it is so great you will never fully understand it. Then you will be filled with the fullness of life and power that comes from God!

[20] Now glory be to God! By His mighty power at work within us, he is able to accomplish infinitely more than we would ever dare to ask or hope.

EPHESIANS 3:17-20 NLT[1]

Chapter 13

ABUNDANTLY FREE

*⁷Because of the sacrifice of the Messiah, his blood poured out on the altar of the Cross, we're a free people — free of penalties and punishments chalked up by all our misdeeds. And not just barely free, either. **Abundantly free!** ⁸He thought of everything, provided for everything we could possibly need, ⁹letting us in on the plans he took such delight in making.*

EPHESIANS 1:7-8 MSG

As I read this passage of Scripture, the revelation of God's love fills my heart to such a degree that tears fill my eyes. My heart is filled with love toward my Savior Who demonstrated such unconditional love toward me. Through His one sacrifice on the cross, Jesus set us free from all the penalties and punishments we deserve because of our failures. As a result, when we put our trust in Him, we don't have to pay for our sins anymore because He has already paid the price for us. And we're not just barely free either, we're abundantly free! Free from the shame and condemnation that sin brings to our hearts. We're free to truly live loved by Him!

The opposite of this freedom is condemnation, which is a negative opinion of yourself. It comes as the result of believing the devil's lie that **you're not who God says you are** because of your failures. It's the belief in your heart that you really don't deserve God's blessing because you haven't been good enough. Condemnation and shame bring fear to our hearts which causes us to question whether or not our Heavenly Father really will answer our prayers and fulfill His promises in our lives.

I used to live in condemnation because I believed the devil's lies. Shame was deeply imbedded in my heart. My heart was filled with fear because I was unsure of my Heavenly Father's opinion of me. But thank goodness, I no longer live there. Today I am free to receive His unconditional love and blessings because my heart has come to believe the truth that there is no condemnation to those of us who are in Christ Jesus!

Romans 8:1, 29-34 and 38-39:

¹Therefore, [there is] now no condemnation (no adjudging guilty of wrong) for those who are in Christ Jesus. AMP

²⁹For those whom He foreknew [...and loved beforehand], He also destined from the beginning... to be molded into the image of His Son [and share inwardly His likeness], that He might become the firstborn among many brethren. ³⁰And those whom He thus foreordained, He also called; and those whom He called, He also justified (acquitted, made righteous, putting them into right standing with Himself). And those whom He justified, He also glorified.

³¹What then shall we say to [all] this? If God is for us, who [can be] against us? [Who can be our foe, if God is on our side?] ³²He who did not withhold or spare [even] His own Son but gave Him up for us all, will He not also with Him freely and graciously give us all [other] things? ³³Who shall bring any charge against God's elect [when it is] God Who justifies [...Who puts us in right relation to Himself? Who shall come forward and accuse or impeach those whom God has chosen? Will God, Who acquits us?] ³⁴Who is there to condemn [us]? Will Christ Jesus... Who died, or rather Who was raised from the dead, Who is at the right hand of God actually pleading as He intercedes for us? AMP

³⁸And I am convinced that nothing can ever separate us from his love. Death can't, and life can't. The angels can't, and the demons can't. Our fears for today, our worries about tomorrow, and even the powers of hell can't keep God's love away. ³⁹Whether we are high above the sky or in the deepest ocean, nothing in all creation will ever be able to separate us from the love of God that is revealed in Christ Jesus our Lord. NLT¹

When I read this I have to just stop and say, "WOOHOO!" Jesus made it possible for you and me to live abundantly free from shame and condemnation by receiving our Heavenly Father's unconditional love toward us, and His good opinion of us in Christ. I love verse 33 in which Paul asks, *"Who can bring a charge against us?"* If our Heavenly

Father, the King of kings, judges us justified, acquitted, innocent, and righteous, then no other judgment matters. He is the final authority in our lives. What He says about us is true!

Verse 34 says that Jesus is sitting at the right hand of the Father, actually pleading your case for *you*. Jesus is your advocate.

1 John 2:1-2:
> *¹My little children, I write you these things so that you may not violate God's law and sin. But if anyone should sin, we have an Advocate (One Who will intercede for us) with the Father—[it is] Jesus Christ [the all] righteous [upright, just, Who conforms to the Father's will in every purpose, thought, and action]. ²And He [that same Jesus Himself] is the propitiation (the atoning sacrifice) for our sins, and not for ours alone but also for [the sins of] the whole world. AMP*

The Apostle John is admonishing you in this verse not to sin, but if you do sin, Jesus is at the right hand of the Father interceding for you. His sacrifice was enough to free you from all condemnation. Even when you fail, He is constantly reminding you that you are righteous in Him.

One day while I was asking the Lord for a deeper revelation of this truth, an illustration of a courtroom scene came into my mind. It was so powerful and it helped me understand what it means for Jesus to be sitting at the right hand of the Father, interceding on my behalf.

The Father is the Righteous Judge (2 Timothy 4:8). The Bible says that the devil is your accuser (Revelation 12:10), and he is the prosecuting attorney. Jesus is your advocate and defense attorney. He sits at the right hand of the Father, interceding for you, and you are seated with Him (Ephesians 2:6).

IMAGINE YOURSELF AS THE DEFENDANT IN THE FOLLOWING COURTROOM SCENE

You are seated on the witness stand. The devil is the prosecuting attorney, throwing his fiery darts of accusation at your heart. He takes the Law, the very Word of God and begins to accuse you, saying, "You are not righteous. The law says you have to keep all of God's commands perfectly in order to be declared righteous (Deuteronomy 6:24-25). *You* have failed so many times, you don't even come close to measuring up!"

Jesus, who sits at the right hand of the Father begins to speak to you as He pleads your case to the Father. You hear Him say, "I am the atoning sacrifice for all your sins. Although the Law could never make you righteous, I love you so much that I died and rose again so that you could be declared righteous in Me. I have fulfilled the law for you and given you My righteousness as a gift of grace. You are righteous because of your faith in Me!" (Romans 3:20-24)

The Father slams His gavel down on the desk and boldly states to you, "You have been declared righteous in my sight, not because you have obeyed the Law perfectly, but because *you have placed your faith in my Son, Jesus.*"

The devil speaks to your heart again with another accusation, "There are many conditions to God's promises and *you* have not met them all. The Law says *you* have to obey all God's commands perfectly in order to be blessed by Him (Deuteronomy 28:1-14) and we all know *you* have failed to meet this condition. *You* do not qualify for God's promised blessings!"

Jesus, your Advocate, defends you again, "You are no longer a slave to the law and its demands upon you. *You are my Father's beloved child* and an heir to all of His promises. You qualify for all My Father's promised blessings because you have been made righteous through your faith in Me." (Galatians 4:4-7; Colossians 1:12-14)

The Father slams his gavel on his desk again and says to you, "You are My beloved child and everything I have belongs to you. My promised blessings are 'Yes' and 'Amen' in your life because you are in My Son, Jesus!" (2 Corinthians 1:20)

The devil makes one more attempt to accuse you and fill your heart with condemnation, He looks at you saying, "You are guilty of many sins. Yesterday, you argued with your spouse and were impatient with your children. You have made many poor choices in the past. The Law says, 'If you do not obey every command of God, you'll be cursed'. (Deuteronomy 28:15-66) You deserve the curse and must pay for your sins."

Sitting at the right hand of the Father, Jesus once

again says to you, "I purchased your freedom from the curse of the law by becoming a curse for you (Galatians 3:13-14). Your sins are forgiven and you are abundantly free from the penalty and punishments chalked up by your misdeeds (Ephesians 1:7). You are free from condemnation because of your faith in Me."

The Father slams his gavel down one last time and forever declares to you, "I don't remember a sin you ever committed (Hebrews 8:12). I have established a New Covenant. Because of your faith in My Son, Jesus, I judge you forgiven, justified, innocent, acquitted, and righteous in Him. There is no condemnation for you because you are in Christ Jesus!"

What a powerful illustration of what it means for Jesus to intercede on your behalf. The Father, Son, and Holy Spirit all agree that you have been made righteous and free from all condemnation through your faith in Jesus. The question is who are you agreeing with: your accuser or the One Who loves you? Your answer to this question is what determines whether or not you experience the freedom that Jesus purchased for you.

For many years of my Christian life my heart was filled with shame because as a teenager I got pregnant before I was married. For the first seven years of my marriage I struggled with discouragement and disappointment because of the devil's accusations against me. These are the lies he spoke to my heart, "You don't deserve a happy marriage because of the sin that you committed. You have to pay for your sin. God won't bless your marriage," and I believed them. I experienced this shame even though the Father, Son and Holy Spirit had already agreed that I had been forgiven and justified through my faith in Jesus. My freedom had been purchased with Jesus' blood. For years I lived in bondage to condemnation and guilt because I believed the lies of my accuser. My heart believed I was guilty as charged.

Do you see how a Christian who has been set free by being declared forgiven, justified, righteous and innocent by the King of kings can still live in bondage? It's because they agree with their accuser.

It wasn't until I finally cried out to Jesus to "show me the truth that will set me free," that the Holy Spirit began to give me a revelation of God's amazing love and grace. This is what He spoke to my heart, "Connie, I declare you justified. Your sins are forgiven and forgotten. You don't have to pay anymore. I made you righteous and worthy of all My promised blessings through your faith in Jesus! I paid the price for you to live loved! I paid the price for you to live free!"

So, how can we live free from our past mistakes? Look at what the Lord says: [18]*"Forget the former things; do not dwell on the past.* [25]*I, even I, am he who blots out your transgressions, for my own sake, and remembers your sins no more."* (Isaiah 43:18, 25 NIV)

[22]*"I have swept away your sins like the morning mists. I have scattered your offenses like the clouds. Oh, return to me, for I have paid the price to set you free."* (Isaiah 44:22 NLT [1])

As I surrendered the lies I believed and embraced the truth of what my Savior had done for me, my heart was set free from condemnation and my whole life began to be transformed. The more I thought upon the truth of who I am in Jesus and His great love for me, the more freedom I began to walk in. I found myself experiencing the blessing of God upon my life as I began to agree with the One Who loves me.

Remember, who you choose to agree with will determine which plan you'll experience in your life. Do you want to live in bondage or freedom? The choice is yours! The price for your freedom has already been paid. You can live abundantly free from condemnation and experience God's abundant blessings by agreeing with the One Who loves you! Establish your heart in the truth by saying, "Lord, I agree with You! Thank You for setting me free from all guilt and condemnation. My sins have been forgiven and forgotten. I am righteous, justified, innocent, and acquitted from all the charges against me because of Your great sacrifice! I am now free to live in Your love!"

Chapter 14

THE DEVIL HAS BEEN DISARMED

⁷I'm leaping and singing in the circle of your love; you saw my pain, you disarmed my tormentors...

PSALM 31:7 MSG

Remember the courtroom scene in the last chapter? What did the devil use to accuse and build his case against you? The devil uses the law to accuse you and prove that you and I are not righteous nor worthy of God's blessing. If we were still under the law, his accusations about us would be true. But the Good News is that we who have accepted Jesus as our Savior are no longer under the jurisdiction of the law; instead, we are under God's grace (Romans 6:14). Our failures to uphold the law, which our accuser uses against us, have been nailed to the cross. Our prosecuting attorney has been disarmed. His evidence is not valid; he has nothing on us and is just blowing smoke. When we know who we are in Jesus and what He accomplished for us on the cross, the devil can no longer accuse us of not being good enough, nor deceive us with his lies.

Colossians 2:10-16, 18:

> *¹⁰You also are complete through your union with Christ...¹¹When you came to Christ, you were "circumcised," but not by a physical procedure. Christ performed a spiritual circumcision—the cutting away of your sinful nature.*

¹²For you were buried with Christ when you were baptized. And with him you were raised to new life because you trusted the mighty power of God, who raised Christ from the dead. ¹³You were dead because of your sins and because your sinful nature was not yet cut away. Then God made you alive with Christ, for he forgave all our sins. ¹⁴He canceled the record of the charges against us and took it away by nailing it to the cross. ¹⁵In this way, he disarmed the spiritual rulers and authorities. He shamed them publicly by his victory over them on the cross. ¹⁶So don't let anyone condemn you.

¹⁸Let no one defraud you by acting as an umpire and declaring you unworthy, and disqualifying you for the prize. NLT²

You and I were once sinners. The law condemned us and proved that we were sinners because we failed to uphold God's commands. When we came to Christ however, our old sinful nature was cut away from us and Jesus gave us a brand new righteous nature by forgiving all our sins. The record of the charges against us, which proved that we were sinners, was nailed to the cross. You and I are no longer defined by our failures; instead we are defined by our new nature in Christ. The devil has been completely disarmed because he can't use our failures against us anymore. When we receive God's forgiveness in Christ, it frees us from all shame and condemnation. As verses 16 and 18 admonish, let no one condemn you! Let no one deceive you by disqualifying you for God's blessing. You have been qualified in Christ!

To continue living free from condemnation and the devil's accusations we must remember this truth when we fail. The devil is just waiting for you to fail so that he can come and accuse you again. He hopes that you'll forget who you are and receive condemnation and shame in your heart.

Shortly after the Holy Spirit revealed this wonderful Good News to me from Colossians 2:10-18, I had the opportunity to apply it to my life. One morning, while getting ready to teach my weekly Bible Study, I got very angry with my husband and began arguing with him. Without realizing it, I had fallen into sin by entering into strife with him. Frustrated, I stormed out of his office, went into my bedroom and cried.

This incident was my accuser's opportunity to condemn me, and he began hurling his accusations against me saying, "Look at you! You don't qualify to teach Bible study. You just disobeyed God. You're a failure!" I thought about His accusations briefly, then turned to Jesus and said, "Jesus, help me! I'm sorry I didn't trust You and I got into strife with my husband. Remind me one more time of the truth that sets me free."

At that moment Colossians 2:13-18 came up in my heart, the Holy Spirit reminding me that my failures, which had disqualified me for God's blessing, were now nailed to the cross. The devil had been disarmed. His accusations against me had no merit: they were all lies.

THE HOLY SPIRIT MINISTERED THE TRUTH TO MY HEART AND POINTED ME TO JESUS

I heard Jesus say, "Connie, your sins are forgiven. You are righteous in Me. You're qualified and anointed to teach God's Word because of who you are in Me. Don't let the devil or anyone else deceive you into believing that you are unworthy or disqualified for my blessing." As I agreed with the truth, God's love set my heart free from condemnation.

As you learn to live free from condemnation, you will find yourself being used by God to set others free as well. Empowered by the Holy Spirit, I boldly said to the devil, "You have nothing on me! You are the one who is going to pay! I'm going to Bible Study today and teach those ladies that you have been disarmed. Your accusations against them are all lies. They are going to be equipped with the truth that the charges against them have been nailed to the cross. They will live free from condemnation by realizing they are forgiven and qualified in Jesus!" I felt so empowered to share this Good News with others!

Later that day, my husband and I peacefully discussed the situation which had earlier made me angry. As I received God's forgiveness for myself and walked free from condemnation, I was empowered by the Holy Spirit to forgive my husband and to love Him with God's love. The devil had lost and his plan did not come to pass in my life because I agreed with the One Who loves me. That's what it looks like to live loved and live free.

When you agree with the accusations of the devil and your heart is filled with condemnation, you will also agree with his accusations toward others. On the other hand, when you live free from condemnation by embracing your Heavenly Father's opinion of you, the main fruit of your life is love. The Holy Spirit will empower you to love others in the same way that Jesus loves you. Your heart will be free from all negative emotions toward yourself and others when it is filled with the truth that you are loved!

The next time you fail and the devil begins accusing your heart, remember he has been disarmed. Any charges he tries to make against you have been nailed to the cross. Receive God's forgiveness and remember that you are the righteousness of God in Christ Jesus. Live loved and live free by agreeing with the One Who loves you!

Chapter 15

THE GIFT OF NO CONDEMNATION

17For God did not send the Son into the world in order to judge (to reject, to condemn, to pass sentence on) the world, but that the world might find salvation and be made safe and sound through Him. 18He who believes in Him [who clings to, trusts in, relies on Him] is not judged [he who trusts in Him never comes up for judgment; for him there is no rejection, no condemnation— he incurs no damnation].

JOHN 3:17-18 AMP

God did not send Jesus into the world to judge and condemn men for their sins. He sent Jesus so that the world might find salvation and freedom from sin through trusting Him. The Good News is that we who have put our trust in Jesus will never be judged and condemned by Him, and we have the awesome privilege of sharing this Good News with others.

In the last two chapters we've discussed a courtroom scene. You've learned that the devil is your accuser, and Jesus is your advocate. Now we'll read a story from the Bible in which a woman really was on trial for her sin. This passage of Scripture reveals Jesus' heart of love and grace toward those of us who have failed. His gift of no condemnation is made very clear. I pray it touches your heart as it has mine:

John 8:1-11:

> *¹But Jesus went to the Mount of Olives. ²Early in the morning (at dawn), He came back into the temple [court], and the people came to Him in crowds. He sat down and was teaching them, ³when the scribes and Pharisees brought a woman who had been caught in adultery. They made her stand in the middle of the court and put the case before Him.*

> *⁴Teacher, they said, This woman has been caught in the very act of adultery. ⁵Now Moses in the Law commanded us that such [women—offenders] shall be stoned to death. But what do You say [to do with her—what is Your sentence]? ⁶This they said to try (test) Him, hoping they might find a charge on which to accuse Him.*

> *But Jesus stooped down and wrote on the ground with His finger. ⁷However, when they persisted with their question, He raised Himself up and said, Let him who is without sin among you be the first to throw a stone at her. ⁸Then He bent down and went on writing on the ground with His finger.*

> *⁹They listened to Him, and then they began going out, conscience-stricken, one by one, from the oldest down to the last one of them, till Jesus was left alone, with the woman standing there before Him in the center of the court. ¹⁰When Jesus raised Himself up, He said to her, Woman, where are your accusers? Has no man condemned you? ¹¹She answered, No*

one, Lord! And Jesus said, I do not condemn you either. Go on your way and from now on sin no more. AMP

In these verses we see a perfect example of a courtroom scene. The Pharisees brought a woman before Jesus to be judged who was caught in the act of adultery. Just like the devil, the Pharisees used the law to accuse her and prove that she deserved to be condemned for her sin. The law said that her punishment was to be stoned, and the religious leaders wanted to make sure she got what she deserved. They tested Jesus by asking, *"The law says she should be stoned to death, but what do you say?"* They all had stones in their hands which represent the law which brings death (2 Corinthians 3:6). They were ready to pass the judgment of the law on her when Jesus spoke up and said, *"Let him who is without sin cast the first stone."* Jesus revealed a very important truth in this statement: only those who are without sin are qualified to judge someone else. You and I are not qualified to pass judgment on anyone because we have all been guilty of sin. But neither is anyone else qualified to pass judgment on us. The truth is, all of us deserve to be punished according to the law, but thank God for Jesus!

As each of them realized that they too were guilty of sin, they dropped their stones (the law) and walked away. Jesus was the only one without sin. He was the only one qualified to judge this woman, and yet he didn't have a stone (the law) in his hand.

When Jesus and the woman caught in adultery were the

only ones left, He asked this question: *"Woman, where are your accusers? Has no man condemned you?"* She said, *"No, one Lord."* In calling Him Lord, she was acknowledging her faith in Jesus. It was at this moment that Jesus revealed His heart of love and grace toward her.

John 1:17:

> *17 For while the Law was given through Moses, grace (unearned, undeserved favor and spiritual blessing) and truth came through Jesus Christ.* AMP

Looking at this woman with love in His eyes, Jesus said, *"I do not condemn you either. Go on your way and from now on sin no more."*

JESUS SET HER FREE FROM THE PENALTY OF HER SIN BY GIVING HER THE GIFT OF NO CONDEMNATION

When this woman received Jesus' gift of no condemnation for her sins, she then had the power *to go and sin no more.* Many of us have believed the lie that we first have to stop sinning in order to keep ourselves from being condemned. But the exact opposite is true. First we must receive the gift of "no condemnation to those who are in Christ Jesus," which then gives us the power to live a life free from sin.

Have you ever been condemned by yourself or others because of your failures? Has it given you the power to go and sin no more? No. Condemnation keeps you in the vicious cycle of sin, but God's grace sets you free from that cycle.

Have you ever felt condemned and unworthy because of a certain sin in your life? You may have had an addiction, experienced an abortion, been through a divorce, committed adultery, struggled with overeating, mismanaged your money, or fallen into sexual immorality. Perhaps you are serving a prison sentence for a crime you committed; or you may just struggle with feelings of guilt and condemnation because of your failures.

The devil and the teachers of the law accuse and condemn you by judging you unworthy of God's approval and blessing, but that's not Jesus' heart towards you. In the same way that Jesus extended His grace toward this woman who was caught in adultery, He also extends His grace toward you. He wants you to live free from sin, so He offers you the same gift he gave to this woman. As you stand before your Savior, let His words of love penetrate deep within your heart and set you free. Hear him say to you, "My beloved, I do not condemn you, go and sin no more." As you listen, how do Jesus' words of love and his gift of no condemnation affect your heart? By receiving His gift of no condemnation, you are living loved. This gift is what empowers you to live free from sin (Romans 5:17). This is the abundant life Jesus came to give you! You are free to live loved by Him!

PART 6

AMAZING GRACE

17 May Christ through your faith [actually] dwell (settle down, abide, make His permanent home) in your hearts! May you be rooted deep in love and founded securely on love, 18 that you may have the power and be strong to apprehend and grasp with all the saints [God's devoted people, the experience of that love] what is the breadth and length and height and depth [of it]; 19 [that you may really come] to know [practically, through experience for yourselves] the love of Christ, which far surpasses mere knowledge [without experience]; that you may be filled [through all your being] unto all the fullness of God [may have the richest measure of the divine Presence, and become a body wholly filled and flooded with God Himself]!

20 Now to Him Who, by (in consequence of) the [action of His] power that is at work within us, is able to [carry out His purpose and] do superabundantly, far over and above all that we [dare] ask or think [infinitely beyond our highest prayers, desires, thoughts, hopes, or dreams] — 21 To Him be glory in the church and in Christ Jesus throughout all generations forever and ever.
Amen (so be it).

EPHESIANS 3:17-21 AMP

Chapter 16

AMAZING GRACE

*[17]For while the law was given through Moses,
grace (unearned, undeserved favor
and spiritual blessing)
and truth came through Jesus Christ.*
JOHN 1:17 AMP

In my journey of living loved and living free, one of the things that has absolutely changed my life is the understanding of what it means to no longer live under the law, but rather to live in God's grace. The Bible says that the law condemns and kills, but the Spirit of grace gives life (2 Corinthians 3:6). At one time, we were all in bondage to the law, but Jesus came to set us free. The Bible says that the law was given by Moses, but something very different — grace and truth — came through Jesus Christ.

The law requires that you earn God's blessing and favor through your perfect obedience to His commands, and then gives you what you deserve based on your actions. Grace, on the other hand, is the unearned, undeserved favor and blessing of God based on your faith in Jesus. Galatians 5:1 says, *So Christ has really set us free...don't get tied up again in slavery to the law.* NLT[1] Those who live under the law live in bondage, but those who learn to live in God's grace truly live loved and live free!

Ephesians 2:1-10:

[1]Once you were dead, doomed forever because of your many sins. [2]You used to live just like the rest of the world, full of sin, obeying Satan, the mighty prince of the power of the air. He is the spirit at work in the hearts of those who refuse to obey God. [3]All of us used to live that way, following the passions and desires of our evil nature. We were born with an evil nature, and we were under God's anger just like everyone else. NLT[1]

*[4]But God — so rich is He in His mercy! Because of and in order to satisfy the great and wonderful and intense love with which He loved us, [5]even when we were dead... by [our own] shortcomings and trespasses, He made us alive together in fellowship and in union with Christ;[... for] **it is by grace** (His favor and mercy which you did not deserve) that you are saved (**delivered from judgment and made partakers of Christ's salvation**).*

*[6]And He raised us up together with Him and **made us sit down together [giving us joint seating with Him]** in the heavenly sphere [by virtue of our **being**] **in Christ Jesus**.... [7]He did this that He might clearly demonstrate through the ages to come the immeasurable (limitless, surpassing) riches of **His free grace (His unmerited favor)** in [His] kindness and goodness of heart toward us in Christ Jesus.*

*[8]For it is **by free grace (God's unmerited favor)** that you are saved (**delivered from judgment and***

made partakers of Christ's salvation) through [your] faith. And this salvation is not of yourselves [of your own doing, it came not through your own striving], but it is the gift of God; ⁹Not because of works [not the fulfillment of the Law's demands], lest any man should boast. [It is not the result of what anyone can possibly do, so no one can pride himself in it or take glory to himself.]

¹⁰For we are God's [own] handiwork (His workmanship), recreated in Christ Jesus...that we may do those good works which God predestined (planned beforehand) for us [taking paths which He prepared ahead of time], that we should walk in them [living the good life which He prearranged and made ready for us to live]." AMP

When I read this passage of Scripture, my heart is overwhelmed with love and thanksgiving toward Jesus for what He accomplished for you and me on the cross. The magnitude of His great, wonderful and intense love for us has become very real to my heart. You see, you and I used to be dead in our sins. We were doomed to failure and disappointment, with a sinful nature just like the rest of mankind.

But in order to satisfy his great, wonderful, and intense love, even when we were dead in our sins, our Heavenly Father made us alive in Christ. By His grace — His unearned favor and undeserved blessing — He saved us from the judgment of our sins and raised us up together with Jesus. He gave us the position of highest honor by seating us with Jesus and making us one with Him.

Hebrews 12:2:

> *[2][Jesus] is seated in the place of highest honor beside God's throne in heaven. NLT[1]*

Ephesians 2:6:

> *[6]For he raised us from the dead along with Christ, and we are seated with him in the heavenly realms — all because we are one with Christ Jesus. NLT[1]*

This is your new position in Christ. Your Heavenly Father honors and esteems you in the very same way He honors and esteems Jesus because you have been made one with Jesus. You are in Him and He is in you (Galatians 2:20).

Imagine the throne of God, with Jesus sitting on the right hand of the Father in the highest place of honor, and you seated in Him because you have been made one with Him by the grace of God. You, too, are sitting in the highest place of honor in Christ.

WHAT DOES IT MEAN TO BE "IN CHRIST"?
WHAT ARE THE PRIVILEGES OF YOUR POSITION IN HIM?

Because you are in Christ Jesus, Ephesians 1:3 says you are blessed with every spiritual blessing in the heavenly realm. What are these spiritual blessings?

In Christ, you have a brand new nature of love. You are the righteousness of God in Him: 2 Corinthians 5:21

In Christ, you are holy and without fault in your Heavenly Father's eyes: Ephesians 1:4

In Christ, you are the beloved son or daughter of God: Ephesians 1:5

In Christ, you are highly favored, accepted and approved by the Father: Ephesians 1:6

In Christ, you are forgiven and redeemed: Ephesians 1:7

In Christ, you are free from shame and condemnation: Romans 8:1

In Christ, you're a joint heir with Jesus and everything the Father has belongs to you: Galatians 4:5-7

In Christ, you have received an inheritance: Ephesians 1:11

Ephesians 1:9,11:

> *⁹God's secret plan has now been revealed to us; it is a plan centered on Christ... ¹¹because of Christ, we have received an inheritance from God. NLT¹*

Ephesians 3:6:

> *⁶And this is [His] secret plan: The Gentiles have an equal share with the Jews in all the riches inherited by God's children. Both groups have believed the Good News, and both are part of the same body and enjoy together the promise of blessings through Christ Jesus. NLT¹*

In Christ, the Holy Spirit empowers you to walk in righteousness: Ephesians 1:13,19-20

In Christ, every promise of God is *Yes,* and *Amen* in your life: 2 Corinthians 1:20

In Christ, the Father sings over you with joy. You are the delight of His heart: Zephaniah 3:17

What does it do for your heart to realize that you have been placed in the highest position of honor in Christ? You are one with Jesus and a joint heir with Him to all the promised blessings of God because of His amazing grace!

Your Heavenly Father placed you in this highest position of honor to demonstrate His grace (His unmerited favor), goodness and kindness of heart toward you in Christ. You did not earn this honored position through your obedience to the law and its demands on you, so you can't pride yourself in your good works. You were given this position as a gift of God's grace when you placed your faith in Jesus.

I used to believe that my obedience to God's law was what put me in a position of honor and qualified me for God's promised blessings in my life. Because of this kind of thinking, I was always striving to be good enough, continually looking for that one message that would give me the answer to what I needed *to do* in order to qualify. I saw myself as lacking instead of complete in Christ. Without realizing it, I had fallen for the exact same lie that Eve had, which was, *If you do "this" you will be like God.* As a result, I was living like a slave trying to earn God's favor and approval, when all the time I was already seated in the highest place of honor in Christ. My Heavenly Father had already made me just like Jesus through my faith in Him.

For years I lived under the Old Covenant of the law, trying to be made righteous through my good works, and it kept me in bondage, producing condemnation in my heart when I failed, and pride in my heart when I thought I was better than someone else.

Over time I became aware that my salvation (my new position in Christ) did not come through any action on my part; not my striving, not my good works, nor my fulfillment of the Law's demands. There was absolutely nothing I could pride myself in or take glory for; my new position in Christ was purely and completely a gift of God's grace; God's unmerited favor which I did not deserve. I came to see that I am God's masterpiece, recreated as a new person in Christ so that my life would produce good works (Ephesians 2:10), not through my own effort, but through the power of the Holy Spirit at work in me. You and I can live the glorious life Jesus has prepared for us when we begin to live our lives in God's grace.

Today I live loved by thankfully acknowledging my honored position in Christ. I agree with who I am in Jesus not because of anything I did to deserve it, but because of His gift of grace. And not only that, I am free to agree with who my husband, my children, my family, and my brothers and sisters in Christ are, too, because they have received the same gift as me. We are seated together with Christ in the highest place of honor as privileged sons and daughters of the King all because of the amazing grace and love of our Savior.

Chapter 17

SIN HAS LOST ITS POWER

23 For the wages of sin is death, but the free gift of God is eternal life through Christ Jesus our Lord.

ROMANS 6:23 NLT [1]

When we begin to live loved by embracing our new position in Christ, sin loses its power in our lives. Sin destroys people's lives. It destroys families, relationships, our health, and our minds. **Proverbs 14:30** says, *envy, jealousy, and wrath are like rottenness of the bones.* AMP Sin has brought destruction into the lives of the people God loves since the beginning of time. From Adam and Eve until now we can see how the world is full of heartache and pain because that is the wage that sin pays; but God loved us so much that He sent Jesus to break the power of sin over our lives so we could live free in His grace.

Romans 5:18-21:

> *18 Yes, Adam's one sin brings condemnation for everyone, but Christ's one act of righteousness brings a right relationship with God and new life for everyone. 19 Because one person disobeyed God, many became sinners. But because one other person obeyed God, many will be made righteous. 20 God's law was given so that all people could see how sinful they were. But as people sinned more and more, God's wonderful grace became more*

abundant. [21] So just as sin ruled over all people and brought them to death, now God's wonderful grace rules instead, giving us right standing with God and resulting in eternal life through Jesus Christ our Lord. NLT [2]

When Adam sinned it brought condemnation to everyone because we all inherited a sinful nature. But when Jesus obeyed God, He made it possible for you and me to inherit a righteous nature through our faith in Him. God's law was given to show us how sinful we were. Sin once ruled over us and brought us death, but now God's wonderful grace rules over us instead, giving us the gift of righteousness and eternal life through Jesus Christ, our Lord.

Now let's continue reading in Romans 6:1-14:

[1] Well then, should we keep on sinning so that God can show us more and more of his wonderful grace? [2] Of course not! Since we have died to sin, how can we continue to live in it? [3] Or have you forgotten that when we were joined with Christ Jesus in baptism, we joined him in his death? [4] For we died and were buried with Christ by baptism. And just as Christ was raised from the dead by the glorious power of the Father, now we also may live new lives.

[5] Since we have been united with him in his death, we will also be raised to life as he was. [6] We know that our old sinful selves were crucified with Christ so that sin might lose its power in our lives. We are no longer slaves to sin. [7] For when we died

with Christ we were set free from the power of sin. ⁸And since we died with Christ, we know we will also live with him. ⁹We are sure of this because Christ was raised from the dead, and he will never die again. Death no longer has any power over him. ¹⁰When he died, he died once to break the power of sin. But now that he lives, he lives for the glory of God.

¹¹So you also should consider yourselves to be dead to the power of sin and alive to God through Christ Jesus. ¹²Do not let sin control the way you live; do not give in to sinful desires. ¹³Do not let any part of your body become an instrument of evil to serve sin. Instead, give yourselves completely to God, for you were dead, but now you have new life. So use your whole body as an instrument to do what is right for the glory of God. ¹⁴Sin is no longer your master, for you no longer live under the requirements of the law. Instead, you live under the freedom of God's grace. NLT ²

I love this passage of Scripture. When some people hear the message of grace—that we are made righteous not through our obedience to the law but through our faith in Christ—they often misunderstand it as an excuse to live in their old sinful nature.

Galatians 5:13:

¹³You have been called to live in freedom — not freedom to satisfy your sinful nature, but freedom to serve one another in love. NLT ¹

You and I have been made free to live loved and to love others with God's unconditional love. That's true freedom!

I personally don't want to have an excuse to act ungodly and live a brokenhearted life. I am convinced that the wages that sin pays is a broken heart and a broken life. I don't want to go down that path and find myself eating with the pigs. I want to agree with what my Heavenly Father says about me and find myself truly free from sin and its effects on my heart and life. I want to live in the freedom of having the power to truly obey God out of a heart that knows I am loved!

The Apostle Paul asked in Romans 6:1:

> *¹Should we keep on sinning so that God can continue to show us more and more of His wonderful grace? Of course not! Since we have died to sin, how can we continue to live in it?* NLT²

Verse 6 says your old sinful self was crucified with Christ so that sin might lose its power in your life. You are no longer a slave to sin. When you died with Jesus, sin lost its power in your life because that's not who you are any more. Your identity is no longer that of a sinner. Your old sinful self, who was angry, offended, resentful, impatient, prideful, selfish, irritable, grouchy, jealous, judgmental, self-indulgent, and fearful died two thousand years ago on the cross with Jesus. You are better than that now! You were raised with Jesus to a brand new life of righteousness. You have a new nature that is loving, kind, joyful, patient, forgiving, humble, compassionate, faithful, self-controlled and peaceful. You are just like Jesus! (Colossians 3:5-15;

Ephesians 4:21-32). When you and I consider ourselves dead to the power of sin and alive in Christ, sin loses its power in our lives.

Titus 2:11-14:

> *11For the grace of God that brings salvation has appeared to all men. 12It teaches us to say "No" to ungodliness and worldly passions, and to live self-controlled, upright and godly lives in this present age, 13while we wait for the blessed hope—the glorious appearing of our great God and Savior, Jesus Christ, 14who gave himself for us to redeem us from all wickedness and to purify for himself a people that are his very own, eager to do what is good.* NIV

God's grace teaches us to say no to sin because it is not a part of who we are anymore. That is our old life that died with Jesus. Jesus gave Himself to purchase our freedom from sin and its evil deeds so that we could live as sons and daughters of God, eager to do what is good.

The other day I was tempted to become very irritated with a particular person in my life, but God's grace has taught me to say no to sin. I remember thinking, *No, that's not who I am anymore, my old sinful self died with Jesus and sin has lost its power in my life. I am the righteousness of God in Christ Jesus and I think only the best about this person. I have the mind of Christ.* I said, "Lord, thank You for Your grace that sets me free!" Immediately, I felt the power of God's grace working in my heart and I began to ponder on that which is good and lovely about them. I felt God's love rise up in my heart toward them. God's grace set my heart free from sin.

I have been tempted to be jealous, offended, judgmental, and fearful at times. I know that if I allow sin in my heart by forgetting who I am in Jesus, it will bring heartache and disappointment into my life. So I constantly take my heart to Jesus and ask for His grace. He reminds me of who I am in Him and empowers me to say no to sin. I am consciously aware that negative thoughts and attitudes are not a part of who I am in Christ. You and I have been given a brand new life in Jesus. When we consider that we are dead to sin and alive to righteousness, sin loses its power in our lives. Grace empowers us to live free from all sin.

WHAT IS TRUE FREEDOM?

Romans 6:15-23:

> ¹⁵*So, since we're out from under the old tyranny, does that mean we can live any old way we want? Since we're free in the freedom of God, can we do anything that comes to mind?* ¹⁶*Hardly. You know well enough from your own experience that there are some acts of so-called freedom that destroy freedom. Offer yourselves to sin, for instance, and it's your last free act.* **But offer yourselves to the ways of God and the freedom never quits.** *All your lives you've let sin tell you what to do.*
>
> ¹⁷*But thank God you've started listening to a new master,* ¹⁸*one whose commands set you free to live openly in his freedom!* ¹⁹*I'm using this freedom language because it's easy to picture. You can*

*readily recall, can't you, how at one time the more you did just what you felt like doing—not caring about others, not caring about God—the worse your life became and the less freedom you had? **And how much different is it now as you live in God's freedom, your lives healed and expansive in holiness?** [20] As long as you did what you felt like doing, ignoring God, you didn't have to bother with right thinking or right living, or right anything for that matter. [21] But do you call that a free life? What did you get out of it? Nothing you're proud of now. Where did it get you? A dead end.*

*[22] But now that you've found you don't have to listen to sin tell you what to do, and have discovered the delight of listening to God telling you, what a surprise! A whole, healed, put-together life right now, with more and more of life on the way! [23] Work hard for sin your whole life and your pension is death. **But God's gift is real life, eternal life, delivered by Jesus, our Master.*** MSG

Sin brings brokenness, bondage and shame to your heart, but Jesus paid the price to set you free to live a whole, healed, put together life that's expansive in freedom. The power to live free from sin and its consequences is found in embracing the truth that you are dead to sin and alive to Jesus. Your sinful nature is dead and buried and your new righteous nature is alive and free.

Sin has lost its power in your life! Believe who you are in Jesus, say no to sin, and live in the freedom of God's amazing grace! Live loved and live free!

Chapter 18

GRACE: THE POWER TO LIVE FREE FROM SIN

My life has been totally transformed by understanding the amazing love and grace of my Savior. I have taught on grace so many times, and yet this wonderful Good News never gets old. The more I think upon it, the deeper and wider my roots go down into God's amazing love for me.

I also know what it feels like to live in the bondage of sin, my heart broken, trying desperately to satisfy my feeling of lack. There is nothing more disheartening than the pain of guilt and shame, and that low-grade fear that never seems to leave. I have felt condemned one minute and self-righteous the next, putting up a good front for everyone to see, but believing that the real me was a failure underneath. I have known the frustration of blame-shifting and judging others, in a futile attempt to feel better about myself.

But now I know what it feels like to live in the freedom of God's grace, my heart whole, embracing the truth that I am complete in Jesus. There is nothing more exhilarating than freedom from all guilt and shame, and the perfect peace that passes all understanding. I love living free from condemnation and pride, realizing that I've been made righteous in Jesus, knowing it has nothing to do with my good works. Because of God's grace, my heart has been filled with love and compassion toward others and a desire for them to experience this same love of Jesus, so that they too, can live loved and free!

Our Heavenly Father knows the pain sin brings to the hearts of his sons and daughters, but He loves us so much that He made a way for us to live free — every single day — by receiving His amazing grace.

GRACE: THE DIVINE INFLUENCE UPON THE HEART AND ITS REFLECTION IN THE LIFE

In the New Testament, the word *grace* comes from the Greek word *charis (Strong's 5485)*. Strong's concordance defines this word as, "the divine influence upon the heart and its reflection in the life." In other words, grace is the Holy Spirit's influence upon your mind, will, and emotions that causes you to reflect your new nature in Christ. Hebrews 10:29 calls the Holy Spirit, *the Spirit of grace*. In the Amplified Bible, 2 Corinthians 1:12 gives another wonderful definition of grace and how it affects your life: *the grace of God (the unmerited favor and merciful kindness by which God exerting His holy influence upon souls, turns them to Christ, and keeps, strengthens, and increases them in Christian virtues).*

What a wonderful definition of grace. It is the Holy Spirit exerting His Holy influence upon your heart that strengthens you to believe the truth and brings out the fruit of righteousness in your life.

In the Old Covenant obedience was a requirement. You had to try hard to obey God. But in the New Covenant of grace, obedience becomes a promise. The Holy Spirit empowers you to obey God when you trust in His power within you. Look at what God promises to do in you through the power of the Holy Spirit:

Philippians 2:13:

> *13 "[Not in your own strength] for it is God Who is all the while effectually at work in you [energizing and creating in you the power and desire], both to will and to work for His good pleasure and satisfaction and delight." AMP*

Galatians 5:22-23:

> *22 "But the fruit of the [Holy] Spirit [the work which His presence within accomplishes] is love, joy (gladness), peace, patience (an even temper, forbearance), kindness, goodness (benevolence), faithfulness, 23gentleness (meekness, humility), self-control (self-restraint, continence). Against such things there is no law [that can bring a charge]." AMP*

I used to struggle to do the right thing. I wanted so badly to obey God, but I always seemed to fail. I lived in the vicious cycle of sin and shame because I did not understand the power of God's grace that was available to me. One day the Holy Spirit revealed Philippians 2:13 to me and I realized that I didn't have to struggle anymore. As I agreed with the truth of who I am in Jesus, and looked to Him daily, He would create in me the desire and power to do what pleased Him. Every time I was tempted with a negative thought or attitude, I would take my heart to Jesus and pray, *Lord, thank You for creating in me the desire and power to do what pleases you.*

Trusting in my own effort and ability to obey God only led to failure, but when I began to trust in Jesus and the Holy Spirit's power within me, I began to see the fruit of the Spirit come out in my life. The Bible says that God gives His grace to those who are humble enough to receive it.

James 4:6-7:

> *⁶But He gives us more and more grace (power of the Holy Spirit, to meet this evil tendency and all others fully). That is why He says, God sets Himself against the proud and haughty, but gives grace [continually] to the lowly (those who are humble enough to receive it). ⁷So be subject to God. Resist the devil [stand firm against him], and he will flee from you. AMP*

James 4:6 defines grace as, *the power of the Holy Spirit, to meet this evil tendency and all others fully.*

The evil tendency that this verse is talking about is self-reliance. It's our tendency to rely upon ourselves instead of Jesus for everything we need. When we rely upon ourselves these other evil tendencies result:

- looking outside of God to meet needs within our heart
- getting angry easily
- being jealous and envious of others
- complaining and nagging
- worry and fear
- getting offended

- being judgmental and critical of others
- being prideful
- being slothful
- unforgiveness and resentment
- being impatient
- being irritable and grouchy

The devil wants to convince your heart that this is who you really are, but that's not true. Remember your old sinful self was crucified with Christ. That's not who you are anymore.

The Holy Spirit meets these evil tendencies. And when grace and sin meet, grace always wins! (Romans 5:21). Sin no longer has power in your life. 2 Corinthians 12:9 says that in your weakness, God's grace makes you strong!

Grace is the power of the Holy Spirit which enables you to overcome every temptation. Grace is not an excuse to live in sin. Instead it's the power of the Holy Spirit that enables you to live a life free from sin (Romans 6:1-14). The one lie the devil is constantly tempting you to believe is: *You're not who God says you are.* He knows that what your heart believes will determine the fruit of your life.

Proverbs 23:7:

> *As [a man] thinks in his heart, so is he.* AMP

If you think you are still your old sinful self with evil tendencies, then you'll remain in bondage to sin. For example, your heart might say, *I have no self-control, I am an angry person. I am so disorganized. I don't have enough faith. I just can't seem to get it right. I can't seem to break free from this addiction. I will always struggle with* _____. **All sin is the result of not believing who you truly are in Christ.** As long as you hold on to that negative opinion of yourself, the vicious cycle of sin and shame will continue in your life, but God's grace is available to set you free.

Whenever you find yourself experiencing negative emotions in your heart, remember the devil is tempting you to believe his lies. Take your heart to Jesus and receive His grace. Talk to Him about how your heart feels and ask Him to show you the truth that will set you free. When you humbly come to the throne of grace, the Holy Spirit will remind you of who you are in Jesus and empower you to believe the truth that sets you free.

Hebrews 4:14-16:

> *" 14Inasmuch then as we have a great High Priest Who has [already] ascended and passed through the heavens, Jesus the Son of God, let us hold fast our confession [of faith in Him]. 15For we do not have a High Priest Who is unable to understand and sympathize and have a shared feeling with our weaknesses and infirmities and liability to the assaults of temptation, but One Who has been tempted in every respect as we are, yet without sinning. 16Let us then fearlessly and confidently and boldly draw near to the throne of grace (the throne of God's unmerited favor to us sinners), that we may receive mercy [for our failures] and find grace*

to help in good time for every need [appropriate help and well-timed help, coming just when we need it]." AMP

This verse encourages you to hold fast to your confession of faith in Jesus: Who are you in Him?

SAY THE TRUTH OUT LOUD. ESTABLISH YOUR HEART IN
THE TRUTH OF WHO YOU ARE IN JESUS:

I am a beloved son or daughter of God — I am valuable in Jesus — I am accepted in Jesus — I am approved in Jesus — I am special and important in Jesus — I am a joint heir with Jesus — I am complete in Jesus — I am seated in the highest place of honor in Jesus — I am righteous in Jesus — I am free from condemnation in Jesus — I am favored and abundantly blessed in Jesus — I am healed in Jesus — I am a success in Jesus — I am an overcomer in Jesus — I am dead to sin and alive to righteousness in Jesus — Sin no longer has any power in my life, in Jesus.

The devil wants you to believe that none of this is true about you.

Romans 5:2,10,17:

²Through [Jesus] also we have... access... by faith into this grace (state of God's favor) in which we [firmly...] stand. And let us rejoice and exult in our hope of experiencing and enjoying the glory of God. ¹⁰For if while we were enemies we were reconciled to God through the death of His Son, it is much more [certain], now that we are reconciled, that we shall be saved (daily delivered from sin's dominion) through His [resurrection] life. [17]*... much more surely will those who receive [God's] overflowing grace... and the free gift of righteousness... reign as kings in life through the one Man Jesus Christ.* AMP

The New Living Translation of **Romans 5:17** says: [17]*All who receive God's wonderful, gracious gift of righteousness will live in triumph over sin and death through this one man, Jesus Christ.* NLT[1]

Romans 5:17 says that when we *receive the gift of righteousness* — who we are in Christ — *and his overflowing grace* — the power of the Holy Spirit — *we will triumph over sin.* We will reign as royal sons and daughters of the King through our faith in Jesus!

PART 7

ABIDING IN HIS LOVE

[16]I pray that from his glorious, unlimited resources he will give you mighty inner strength through his Holy Spirit. [17]And I pray that Christ will be more and more at home in your hearts as you trust in him. May your roots go down deep into the soil of God's marvelous love. [18]And may you have the power to understand, as all God's people should, how wide, how long, how high, and how deep his love really is. [19]May you experience the love of Christ, though it is so great you will never fully understand it. Then you will be filled with the fullness of life and power that comes from God.

[20]Now glory be to God! By his mighty power at work within us, he is able to accomplish infinitely more than we would ever dare to ask or hope. [21]May he be given glory in the church and in Christ Jesus forever and ever through endless ages. Amen.

EPHESIANS 3:16-21 NLT[1]

Chapter 19

TRANSFORMED BY LOVE

*³As I briefly mentioned earlier in this letter, God himself
revealed his secret plan to me. ⁶And this is the secret plan:
The Gentiles have an equal share with the Jews in all
the riches inherited by God's children. Both groups have
believed the Good News, and both are part of the same
body and enjoy together the promise of blessings through
Christ Jesus. ⁸I was chosen for this special joy of telling the
Gentiles about the endless treasures available to them in
Christ. ¹²Because of Christ and our faith in him, we can
now come fearlessly into God's presence,
assured of His glad welcome.*

EPHESIANS 3:3, 6, 8, 12 NLT ¹

There is no greater power in the universe than the power
of love, and God is love! As we learn to live loved by Him,
the power of His love heals our hearts, transforms our lives
and brings glory to His name. I'm sure you've noticed that
we've started each part of this book reading Ephesians
3:17-21. Today we'll take an in-depth look at this powerful
chapter of the Bible.

One day while reading Ephesians chapter 3, verse 8 in
particular stood out to me. I personalize this verse as I
often do when reading Scripture, and I let the truth of it
soak into the depths of my heart. *The Apostle Paul was chosen
for the special joy of telling Connie about the endless treasures
available to her in Christ*, I thought. My mind immediately

went to a wonderful illustration my friend Kelly used with the teenage girls in our Bible Study. She was teaching them about the inner beauty they have because Jesus lives inside them. She brought a jewelry box to our study, filled with hundreds of multi-colored crystal jewels to illustrate her point. Although the outside was plain, the inside was strikingly beautiful as we gazed upon the precious treasures within the box. Each one of those gems represented a treasure we have in Jesus.

Thinking about that powerful lesson one more time and how it relates to this passage of Scripture, I retrieved the jewelry box from my office mantle. Looking at the beautiful treasures it held, I was once again overwhelmed with the love of Jesus. Reaching inside, I picked up a pink gem, watching it glisten in the light. "Father," I asked, "which treasure in Christ does this one represent?" Lovingly, I heard the Father say, "It represents my complete approval of you, my daughter. You don't ever again have to look to another person for approval because you have that treasure in Jesus" (Ephesians 1:6). Tears ran down my face as I pondered how that particular revelation of God's love has transformed my life.

Excited to hear Him speak to my heart again, I picked up a red jewel this time and asked, "Father, which treasure in Christ does this one represent?" He softly answered again, "It represents your value, my daughter. You don't have to prove your value through your performance or anything you do. I proved how valuable you are by paying for you with the blood of My Son, Jesus." (1 Peter 1:18-19)

I could feel my heart being filled with the fullness of God's love as I picked up a purple gem. "Show me once more, Father, what treasure in Christ does this one represent?" "That one represents My gift of righteousness which qualifies you for all of My blessings," He said (2 Corinthians 5:21). "You don't have to struggle to qualify any more, Connie. You can rest in My great love!" Taking in a deep breath, I pondered these treasures I have in Christ and the revelation of God's love within each one that truly sets my heart free. Reaching deep within the jewelry box, I scooped up as many jewels as my hands could hold. As I let them slip out of my fingers and back into the box, I said, "Thank You, Heavenly Father, You have given me so many treasures in Christ; Your love for me is so amazing! What a wonderful life journey I am on, daily discovering the treasures of Your love! I love You so much, Father!"

Sitting in God's presence, I picked up another handful of gems and gazed at them in my hand. The Holy Spirit continued to remind me of the endless treasures available to you and me in Christ: **Peace** (John 16:33); **Joy** (John 15:11); **Favor** (Psalm 5:12); **Protection** (Psalm 91); **Healing** (Isaiah 53:5); **Provision** (Philippians 4:19); **Wisdom** (Ephesians 1:8); **Guidance** (Romans 8:14); **Self-control** (2 Timothy 1:7); **Forgiveness** (Ephesians 1:7); **A Sound Mind** (2 Timothy 1:7); **Freedom from Sin** (Romans 6:6,7); **The power of the Holy Spirit** (Philippians 2:13); **The Mind of Christ** (1 Corinthians 2:16); **Financial Abundance** (2 Corinthians 9:8-11); **A Blessed Family** (Proverbs 3:33); **Blessed Children** (Psalm 112:2); **Acceptance** (Ephesians

1:6); **Deliverance** (Psalm 34:17-19); **A Heart of Love** (Ezekiel 36:26-27); **Security** (Romans 8:38-39); **The Gift of No Condemnation** (Romans 8:1); **Success** (Proverbs 16:3); **Strength** (Philippians 2:13)

Do you realize that every need and desire of your heart has been made available to you in Christ? You are truly complete in Him! His love fills every part of your heart with the fullness of God.

GOD'S LOVE FOR YOU IS REVEALED IN EACH TREASURE THAT HAS BEEN MADE AVAILABLE TO YOU IN CHRIST

Romans 8:39:

> *39Nothing in all creation will ever be able to separate us from the love of God that is revealed in Christ Jesus our Lord. NLT[1]*

After revealing God's secret plan of the treasures made available to us in Christ, the Apostle Paul was inspired by the Holy Spirit to pray for each one of us to know and believe the love that Jesus has for us.

Ephesians 3:14-21:

> *14When I think of the wisdom and scope of God's plan, I fall to my knees and pray to the Father, 15the Creator of everything in heaven and on earth. NLT[1]*
>
> *16I pray that out of his glorious riches he may strengthen you with power through his Spirit in your inner being, 17so that Christ may dwell in your hearts through faith. And I pray that you, being rooted and established in love, 18may have power,*

together with all the saints, to grasp how wide and long and high and deep is the love of Christ, ¹⁹and to know this love that surpasses knowledge — that you may be filled to the measure of all the fullness of God. NIV

²⁰Now to Him Who, by (in consequence of) the [action of His] power that is at work within us, is able to [carry out His purpose and] do super abundantly, far over and above all that we [dare] ask or think [infinitely beyond our highest prayers, desires, thoughts, hopes, or dreams] — ²¹To Him be glory in the church and in Christ Jesus throughout all generations forever and ever. Amen (so be it). AMP

In verses 6 and 8 in Ephesians chapter 3 the Apostle Paul revealed that He was sent to share the Good News of the promise of blessings we all have in Christ. He said the treasures available to us in Christ were endless. In verses 16 and 17, he prayed that the Holy Spirit would strengthen us in our inner man with the power to believe the Good News that He was sent to share with us. He prayed that we'd be strengthened so that Christ might dwell in our hearts through our faith in Him. He prayed that our thoughts and emotions would be filled with Jesus!

I have experienced this great transformation in my heart and life as the Holy Spirit has continued to give me understanding of the riches I have in Christ. He also strengthens me in my inner man with the power to believe

His great love for me. My journey in learning to live loved by Him began by agreeing with the same simple prayer the Apostle Paul was inspired to pray, for you and me. Even now I often pray, "Lord, show me the truth that will set me free. Give me a deeper revelation of Your love for me. Strengthen me by Your grace to believe You."

It is only by the grace of God that we can grasp how wide, long, high and deep the love of Jesus truly is for us. When our hearts are filled with His love, we are filled with the fullness of God. Every need of our heart is fully met. God is able to do exceedingly abundantly above our highest prayers, thoughts, hopes and dreams as we abide in His love.

I have experienced the transforming power of God's love in so many ways, just as it's described in Ephesians 3:16-20. Let me share a personal example. When I first began to teach Bible Study, I was very insecure about talking in front of people. Anytime I got an opportunity to teach, I would worry about what other people thought of me and whether or not I made any sense at all. Each time I'd finish teaching, I would look to people for their approval. If they didn't say anything, I'd think I must not have done a good job. If they did say something encouraging to me, I would think they were just being nice. The enemy would come immediately with this lie, *You're so unqualified to teach anyone.* I would ponder his lies within my heart and it kept me in bondage to insecurity.

I finally got tired of being insecure, and began taking my heart to Jesus concerning this fear. I asked Him to show me the truth that would set me free. The Holy Spirit began revealing to me the treasures I have in Christ:

- I am anointed in Jesus to set the captives free (1 John 2:20,27; Isaiah 61)
- I am qualified in Jesus to deliver the Good News of the Gospel of Grace (2 Corinthians 3:4-6)
- I can do all things through Christ Who strengthens me (Philippians 4:13)

These verses revealed the depth of Christ's love for me in this area of my life. As I pondered the truth in my heart, the Holy Spirit empowered me to believe it. Every time I was tempted to be afraid, I turned to Jesus and asked for strength to believe Him. I thanked Him for His promises of love to me. As a result, my heart has become established and secure in His love. Today I am free from insecurity in this area of my life. I feel empowered by the Holy Spirit to share the Good News of the treasures available to us in Christ.

As the Holy Spirit's power worked in my heart, God was able to bring His purpose to pass in my life. He equipped me to write Bible studies and books. He opened doors for me to travel around the nation and to Russia. He has used me to set the captives free. Now when I stand in front of people, I am very conscious of God's love for me and the treasures I have been given in Christ. God has done far beyond what I hoped or dreamed for in my life. As I have learned to live loved by Him, I have experienced the transforming power of His love.

You too, can experience the transforming power of God's love by thinking upon the treasures available to you in Christ. As you let them penetrate deep within your heart, the power of the Holy Spirit will work in you and you'll experience the freedom Jesus has made available to you through His endless treasures.

Chapter 20

ABIDING IN HIS LOVE

*⁴Dwell in Me, and I will dwell in you. [Live in Me, and I will
live in you.] Just as no branch can bear fruit of itself without
abiding in (being vitally united to) the vine, neither can you
bear fruit unless you abide in Me. ⁵I am the Vine; you are
the branches. Whoever lives in Me and I in him bears much
(abundant) fruit. However, apart from Me [cut off from vital
union with Me] you can do nothing. ⁶If a person does not dwell
in Me, he is thrown out like a [broken-off] branch, and withers;
such branches are gathered up and thrown into the fire,
and they are burned.*

*⁷If you live in Me [abide vitally united to Me] and My words
remain in you and continue to live in your hearts, ask whatever
you will, and it shall be done for you. ⁸When you bear (produce)
much fruit, My Father is honored and glorified, and you show
and prove yourselves to be true followers of Mine.*

*⁹I have loved you, [just] as the Father has loved Me; abide
in My love [continue in His love with Me]. ¹⁰If you keep My
commandments [if you continue to obey My instructions], you
will abide in My love and live on in it, just as I have obeyed
My Father's commandments and live on in His love. ¹¹I have
told you these things, that My joy and delight may be in you, and
that your joy and gladness may be of full measure and complete
and overflowing. ¹²This is My commandment: that you love one
another [just] as I have loved you.*

JOHN 15:4-12 AMP

WHAT DOES IT MEAN TO LIVE AND ABIDE IN THE LOVE OF JESUS AND HOW DOES IT AFFECT YOUR LIFE?

Jesus is the vine and we are the branches. Just as a branch receives everything it needs to flourish and prosper by abiding in the vine, we too, receive everything we need to flourish and prosper through abiding in Jesus. He is our vital necessity. When we abide in Him we bear much abundant fruit, but apart from complete dependence on Him we can do nothing!

JESUS CLEARLY DESCRIBED TWO WAYS IN WHICH WE CAN LIVE

I can totally relate to verse 6 which reveals what happens to a branch that is not abiding in the vine. It does not flourish or prosper; it withers and gets burned. There have been times in my life when I have felt weak, brokenhearted, discouraged, disappointed and fearful because I was depending on either myself or someone else to meet my needs. When I look at myself apart from Jesus, I see myself as lacking in some way.

I can also relate to verses 7 and 8. When I abide in Jesus, thinking upon the treasures I have in Him, His word comes alive in me. I experience peace, joy, and love in my heart, and His promises in my life. When I abide in Jesus, I see myself as complete in Him! In verse 9, Jesus told you that He loves you just like the Father loves Him. He then said to continue to abide in His love. He showed you that the power to love others comes from receiving the Father's love for yourself.

When you read verse 10 which says, *If you keep My commandments... you will abide in my love,* you can mistakenly get the idea that Jesus is saying if you obey His commandments then He will love you. But the commandment Jesus is specifically referring to is found in verse 12, *This is My commandment: that you love one another [just] as I have loved you.* What Jesus is really teaching us in verse 10 is this: if you love others the way Jesus loves you, **you are** abiding in His love.

Look at John 15:9,10,12 again in the Message Bible:

⁹I've loved you the way my Father has loved me. Make yourselves at home in my love. ¹⁰If you keep my commands, you'll remain intimately at home in my love. That's what I've done— kept my Father's commands and made myself at home in his love. ¹²This is my command: Love one another the way I loved you.

Let's recall the ways in which Jesus loves you:

- He forgives and forgets all your sins, and never brings them up again (Hebrews 8:12)
- He does not condemn you nor judge you badly when you fail (Romans 8:1)
- He reminds you of who you are in Him and prays for you (Romans 8:29-34)
- He thinks only the best of you and rejoices in the truth about you (Zephaniah 3:17)
- He's never angry at you, but only feels love and compassion toward you (Isaiah 54:9-10)

꙰ He is kind and patient toward you
(1 Corinthians 13:4)

You can try to love people the way Jesus loves you, but apart from abiding in Him, you can do nothing! For many years I tried to honor, respect and love my husband; but in my own strength it was impossible. I found myself dwelling on his weaknesses and the areas he fell short. Any time I looked to him to meet my needs I always came up wanting. And the sense of lack I felt in my heart only produced the fruit of anger, frustration, resentment and disappointment toward him. I wasn't able to obey Jesus' command because I wasn't abiding in His love for me. Apart from Jesus, I could do nothing! I became like a withered up branch.

My heart changed when I began to live in Jesus and His love for me. Then I began to take the needs of my heart to Jesus, and He began to fill it with His great love. Instead of looking to my husband, I began to look to Jesus for approval, provision, security, joy, peace, and unconditional love.

As the needs of my heart were met in Him, I didn't need to look to my husband anymore. God's love set my heart free and empowered me to think on the good in my husband. Now my heart is filled with God's love towards him and I see him as righteous and blessed in Christ. Because Jesus loves both of us, we are blessed together in Him! I am now able to encourage him with the same encouragement the Holy Spirit has given me. Today, I think my husband is wonderful and I am truly blessed to have him in my life. I love him with all of my heart. Abiding in the love of Jesus transformed my heart and my marriage.

I now talk often to Jesus about His great love for me and think upon the endless treasures I have in Him; the promise of blessings that He purchased for me. It's during these moments that my heart is overwhelmed with His love because He has met every need and desire of my heart. This is what it means to abide in Jesus and remain intimately at home in His love.

Whenever I am tempted to feel irritated and frustrated with anyone, I take my heart to Jesus and let Him fill it with His love once again. I just have to refocus my attention on the One Who loves me and remember who I am in Him. When I abide in His love, my heart is filled with peace, and I am free to love others with His unconditional love.

You too, can live in the freedom of abiding in Jesus and His great love for you. Be conscious everyday that you are complete in Him. Thank Him for His love for you, and think upon the endless treasures you have in Him. Look to Jesus to meet every need of your heart; you won't need to look anywhere else. Doing this will have a positive effect on every relationship in your life. You'll be filled up and overflowing with His love to such a degree that loving others the way He loves you will effortlessly flow from your heart. When you abide in His love, you'll bear much abundant fruit and your Heavenly Father will be glorified in you! His good opinion of you will come shining through!

Chapter 21

THE PRAYER JESUS PRAYED FOR US

[20]Neither for these alone do I pray [it is not for their sake only that I make this request], but also for all those who will ever come to believe in (trust in, cling to, rely on) Me through their word and teaching, [21]That they all may be one, [just] as You, Father, are in Me and I in You, that they also may be one in Us, so that the world may believe and be convinced that You have sent Me.

[22]I have given to them the glory and honor which You have given Me, that they may be one [even] as We are one: [23]I in them and You in Me, in order that they may become one and perfectly united, that the world may know and [definitely] recognize that You sent Me and that You have loved them [even] as You have loved Me.

[24]Father, I desire that they also whom You have entrusted to Me [as Your gift to Me] may be with Me where I am, so that they may see My glory, which You have given Me [Your love gift to Me]; for You loved Me before the foundation of the world.

[25]O just and righteous Father, although the world has not known You and has failed to recognize You and has never acknowledged You, I have known You [continually]; and these men understand and know that You have sent Me. [26]I have made Your Name known to them and revealed Your character and Your very Self, and I will continue to

make [You] known, that the love which You have bestowed
upon Me may be in them [felt in their hearts] and that I
[Myself] may be in them.

JOHN 17:20-26 AMP

As I read the Gospels, I love watching how Jesus interacts with the Father. He demonstrates such dependence and security in His Father's love. That's how I want to live, just like Jesus. Jesus came to reconcile us into the very same relationship with the Father that He had. He wants us to live just like He did in this world. Through the prayer He prayed for us in John 17, He demonstrated what it looks like to abide in our Heavenly Father's love.

What intimacy the Son had with the Father! Jesus established His heart in His Father's love by acknowledging the truth about their relationship. In His prayer, Jesus showed us what it looks like to abide in His Father's love. Let's take a look:

1. Jesus talked to His Father about their oneness and intimacy. In verse 21 He said, *"You, Father, are in Me and I in You."*

2. Jesus received the gift of His Father's glory which was the Father's gift of love to His Son. In verse 24 He said, *24 "Father, I desire that they... may be with Me where I am, so that they may see My glory, which You have given Me [Your love gift to Me];"*

3. Jesus acknowledged that the Father loved Him. In verse 24 He said, *"Father,...You loved me before the foundation of the world."*

The wonderful Good News is that in His prayer Jesus revealed the Father's plan to bring you and me into the intimacy of their love relationship by making us one with them, and one with each other. In verse 21, Jesus prayed that you and I would be one with each other, just as He and His Father are one; that we may also be one with them so that the world would believe that He is real. Read part of Jesus' prayer in John 17 out of the Message Bible:

> *[10]Everything mine is yours, and yours mine, and my life is on display in them. [11]For I'm no longer going to be visible in the world; they'll continue in the world while I return to you. Holy Father, guard them as they pursue this life that you conferred as a gift through me, so they can be one heart and mind as we are one heart and mind. [15]I'm not asking that you take them out of the world but that you guard them from the Evil One. [16]They are no more defined by the world than I am defined by the world. [17]Make them holy — consecrated — with the truth; your word is consecrating truth.*

Because we are one with the Son and the Father, everything we have is His and everything He has is ours (Galatians 4:7). Jesus said that just as the world did not define Him, the world and its opinions and judgments does not define us either. The world gains its identity by seeking the good opinion of others, but our identity comes from the good opinion of our Heavenly Father. We are defined by the truth of who we are in Jesus.

In verse 22, Jesus said that He gave us His glory. What

exactly did Jesus mean when He said that He has given us His glory and honor, the same glory and honor that the Father has given him?

The word *glory* in this verse come from the Greek words *Doxa (Strong's 1391)* and *Doxazo (Strong's 1392)*. According to the *Lexical Aids of the New Testament* these words mean:

- All that is excellent in the divine nature
- The image and character of God
- The opinion which one forms is to recognize, honor, praise, invest with dignity, give anyone esteem or honor by putting him into an honorable position
- The revelation and manifestation of all that God is and has
- God's self-revelation in which He manifests all the goodness that He is

When Jesus gave us His glory, He gave us everything that is excellent in His divine nature. He gave us His very character; His perfect righteousness. This means that the good opinion that the Father had of Jesus, Jesus gave to us. He gave us the same honored position His Father gave to Him by making us one with Himself.

Jesus gave His honored position to each of us so that we could truly be one and perfectly united in heart and mind to Him. Jesus is in us and the Father is in Jesus; we are all one in Him. He did this in order that the whole world would know that the Father loves us just as much as He loves Jesus.

By giving us His glory, Jesus made us all exactly like Himself. He gave each one of us His very character; His very own nature. He made us all just as valuable, important, special, anointed, approved and righteous as He is. We have become a part of God's family by virtue of our being in Christ Jesus. Therefore we no longer need to feel superior or inferior toward each other because we realize that we are all just like Jesus in this world. Now when we compare ourselves with each other, we are comparing ourselves in Christ. We are all equal in Christ, loved equally by our Father, equally blessed and favored by Him. The Father rejoices and delights over you in the same way He rejoices and delights over me. He made us one with each other by making us one with Himself.

As we become conscious of this truth, there is no more judging, jealousy, offense, or division among us. We have all been invited into the circle of love, perfectly loved by our Heavenly Father. As we receive His perfect love, we are empowered to love each other with His perfect love, too.

In Verse 26 we see Jesus saying that He revealed the Father's character to us and will continue to reveal Him to us so that the love the Father bestowed on Him may also be felt in our hearts. From this prayer in John 17 we can see that it has always been the Father's plan for us to enjoy the same intimacy with Him that He and Jesus enjoy. It is the Father's desire for all of us to live in His love.

Take a look at Jesus' prayer on the following page. Learn by His example of what it means to live in the Father's love by acknowledging the truth about your relationship with Him:

> *Father, I am in You and You are in me. You gave me Your glory and honor as Your love gift to me. Thank You for making me righteous in Christ Jesus! Father, I know You love me. You have loved me from the foundation of the world. Thank You for making me one with my brothers and sisters in Christ so that we can love each other with Your perfect love.*

Allow the words of this prayer to soak into your heart. Experience the same level of intimacy with the Father that Jesus had by establishing your heart in His love.

PART 8

PERFECT LOVE CASTS OUT ALL FEAR

¹⁴I bow my knees before the Father of our Lord Jesus Christ.

¹⁶May He grant you out of the rich treasury of His glory to be strengthened and reinforced with mighty power in the inner man by the [Holy] Spirit [Himself indwelling your innermost being and personality]. ¹⁷May Christ through your faith [actually] dwell (settle down, abide, make His permanent home) in your hearts! May you be rooted deep in love and founded securely on love, ¹⁸that you may have the power and be strong to apprehend and grasp with all the saints [God's devoted people, the experience of that love] what is the breadth and length and height and depth [of it]; ¹⁹[that you may really come] to know [practically, through experience for yourselves] the love of Christ, which far surpasses mere knowledge [without experience]; that you may be filled [through all your being] unto all the fullness of God [may have the richest measure of the divine Presence, and become a body wholly filled and flooded with God Himself]!

²⁰Now to Him Who, by (in consequence of) the [action of His] power that is at work within us, is able to [carry out His purpose and] do superabundantly, far over and above all that we [dare] ask or think [infinitely beyond our highest prayers, desires, thoughts, hopes, or dreams] —
²¹To Him be glory in the church and in Christ Jesus throughout all generations forever and ever.
Amen (so be it).

EPHESIANS 3:14, 16-21 AMP

Chapter 22

PERFECT LOVE CASTS OUT ALL FEAR

The devil is constantly throwing his lies at us in an attempt to fill our hearts with fear and worry. When we don't know and believe the love our Heavenly Father has for us, we live our lives with a low-grade fear. Because we are not quite convinced of His love for us, we fear that something bad might happen in our lives.

I used to live in fear: Fear of what people thought of me, fear about my finances, fear of sickness, concerns for my children, fear of failure, fear of harm, even fear of talking in front of people. The root of all my fears was that I wasn't quite sure if God would really take care of the things that concerned me. I was unsure of His love for me.

As I have learned to live loved, my heart has become free from fear. Yes, there are still times I am tempted to be fearful, but now when an anxious feeling comes to my heart, I turn to Jesus and ask Him to show me the truth that will set my heart free. He is always faithful to remind me of His promise, and as I receive His love for me, my heart is filled with peace. His perfect love sets my heart free from all fear every time I look to Him.

1 John 4:16-19:

> *16 And we have known and believed the love that God has for us. God is love, and he who abides in*

love abides in God, and God in him. NKJV

17In this [union and communion with Him] love is brought to completion and attains perfection with us, that we may have confidence for the day of judgment [with assurance and boldness to face Him], because as He is, so are we in this world. AMP

18There is no fear in love; but perfect love casts out fear, because fear involves torment. But he who fears has not been made perfect in love. 19We love Him because He first loved us. NKJV

Verse 16 above shows us that God is love. God's perfect love and fear cannot remain in your heart at the same time. They cannot coexist. His perfect love casts out all your fears.

In the Amplified Bible verse 18 says, *(perfect) love turns fear out of doors and expels every trace of terror!* Any time you experience a low grade-fear it's because His love for you has not been established in your heart and you are believing something about God or yourself that is not true. As you become conscious of your union with Jesus (that you are one with Him), and you fellowship with Him daily, you'll find yourself living free from fear. Verse 17 says that it is through your union and communion with Him that love is brought to perfection in your heart. Your heart becomes established in His love as you live and abide in Him. You are not afraid of judgment. You can come before your Heavenly Father with confidence because your heart is established in the truth that you are just like Jesus in this world. You are the righteousess of God in Him!

YOU ARE NO LONGER A FEARFUL SLAVE, BUT AN HEIR TO ALL OF GOD'S PROMISES

Romans 8:15-17:

> *15For [the Spirit which] you have now received [is] not a spirit of slavery **to put you once more in bondage to fear,** but you have received the Spirit of adoption... in... which we cry, Abba...Father! 16The Spirit Himself... testifies together with our spirit, [assuring us] that we are children of God. 17And if we are [His] children, then we are [His] heirs also; heirs of God and fellow heirs with Christ."* AMP

Every time fear comes at my heart, the Holy Spirit reminds me that I am not a fearful slave and that Jesus has set me free from the bondage of fear by making me a daughter of God. I can cry, "Father, I know You love me. I don't have to be afraid. I am an heir to all of Your promises because of my union with Jesus." In my union and communion with Him, His love is brought to perfection in my soul!

GOD'S PERFECT LOVE IS REVEALED IN JESUS

Romans 8:39:

> *39Whether we are high above the sky or in the deepest ocean, nothing in all creation will ever be able to separate us from **the love of God that is revealed in Christ Jesus our Lord.*** NLT[1]

God's perfect love is revealed to us in the promises we have been given in Jesus. Each promise is a treasure we have in Christ, a revelation of His love.

GOD'S PROMISES ARE "YES" AND "AMEN" IN CHRIST JESUS

2 Corinthians 1:19-20:

> [19] *For Jesus Christ, the Son of God, does not waver between "Yes" and "No." He is the one whom Silas, Timothy, and I preached to you, and as God's ultimate "Yes," he always does what he says.* [20] *For all of God's promises have been fulfilled in Christ with a resounding "Yes!" And through Christ, our "Amen" (which means "Yes") ascends to God for his glory.* NLT [2]

> [20] *For no matter how many promises God has made, they are "Yes" in Christ. And so through him the "Amen" is spoken by us to the glory of God.* NIV

BECAUSE YOU ARE IN CHRIST JESUS, YOUR HEAVENLY FATHER SAYS "YES!" TO ALL OF HIS PROMISES:

Yes! *You are the righteousness of God in Christ Jesus!*
2 Corinthians 5:21

Yes! *I have given My angels charge over you to protect you in all your ways!* Psalm 91

Yes! *You are highly favored and abundantly blessed!*
Psalm 5:11,12; 2 Corinthians 9:8

Yes! *You are qualified and anointed to share the Good News!*
2 Corinthians 3:4-6

Yes! *I accept and approve of you!* Ephesians 1:6

Yes! *You are holy and without fault in My sight!* Ephesians 1:4

Yes! *I create in you the desire and the power to do what pleases Me!* Philippians 2:13

Yes! *I set you free from all sin!* Romans 6:11-14

Yes! *You are forgiven. I don't even remember your sins!* Hebrews 8:12

Yes! *You are free from all condemnation and guilt!* Romans 8:1

Yes! *My plan is to prosper you and give you hope for your future!* Jeremiah 29:11

Yes! *Your children are mighty and blessed upon the earth!* Psalm 112:2

Yes! *I will fulfill the desires of your heart!* Psalm 37:4

Yes! *By My stripes you are healed!* Isaiah 53:5

Yes! *During times of famine, you will have more than enough!* Psalm 37:17-19

Yes! *I will teach your children and give them great peace!* Isaiah 54:13

Yes! *I will deliver you from all your troubles!* Psalm 34:19

Yes! *You hear my voice and are led by My Spirit!* Romans 8:14

Yes! *You are equipped with everything you need to carry out My will!* Hebrews 13:20,21

Yes! *You are complete in Christ. You lack nothing!* Colossians 2:10

What do each of these promises in Christ reveal about your Heavenly Father's heart toward you?

HE LOVES YOU!

Read back over each promise again and let it soak

deep within your heart. Take a moment to ponder on the significance of your union with Christ. It's because you are one with Jesus that God says, "Yes!" to His promises in your life. Because you are in Christ Jesus, you can boldly say, "Amen, Lord! I know You love me! Your promises are true in my life!"

My heart is made free from all fear as I agree with the One Who loves me. I remember one particular occasion when fear tried to grip my heart. It was 2001 and the economy was hit hard and people began losing their jobs. My husband came home one day from work to tell me that he would be losing his job as well. I remember so well the fear that tried to enter my heart as this thought came to my mind, *What are we going to do?*

I picked up my Bible from my night-stand and went downstairs to talk with my Heavenly Father. I remember saying, "Heavenly Father, help me to trust You in this situation." As the Holy Spirit began to remind me of the promises I have in Jesus, I responded by saying, "Father, I know You love me because You said Your plan is to prosper us and to give us hope and a future (Jeremiah 29:11). I know You love me because You promised to cause all grace to abound toward us so that we would have more than enough to meet all our needs (2 Corinthians 9:8-11). I know You love me, Father, because You said that You take care of the birds in the air and You promised to take care of us" (Matthew 6:25-33).

As I continued to speak these promises, my heart became established in the truth that my Heavenly Father says "Yes" to all of His promises in my life because I am in Christ Jesus. All I had to do was receive them by saying, "Amen! Lord, what You say about me is true!" Through my union and communion with Him, His love was brought to completion within my heart. His perfect love cast out all my fears!

God was faithful and over the next few months, my husband started His own business and his income doubled. I experienced God's promise of peace and prosperity simply by agreeing with the One Who loves me.

2 Peter 1:3,4:

> [3]*As we know Jesus better, his divine power gives us everything we need for living a godly life. He has called us to receive His own glory and goodness.* NLT[1]

> [4]*Through these he has given us his very great and precious promises, so that through them you may participate in the divine nature and escape the corruption in the world caused by evil desires.* NIV

Your Heavenly Father has given you everything you need to live a life free from fear. He has called you to receive His glory and goodness. Because He loves you, He has given you His great and precious promises so that you can escape the devil's plan of fear and bondage and partake of His divine nature.

The next time the devil tempts you to worry or be afraid, turn your heart to the Father and talk to Him about His great love for you. Keep in mind that it is through your union and communion with Him that His love is brought to perfection in your heart.

As your heart is established in His love, you'll find yourself confidently coming before Him as you say, "Father, I know You love me because of the promise You've given me in Jesus." As you agree with the Father's promise to you, you'll see yourself living fearlessly, confidently and securely in Jesus, your life glorifying God. Watch as His perfect love casts out all your fears!

Chapter 23

LIVING FEARLESSLY

Jesus lived a fearless life here on the earth, facing every situation He encountered with boldness. Living fearlessly however, does not mean that you never feel fear in your heart. What it does mean is that when you're tempted to worry about something, you look to Jesus and receive His grace to empower you to trust Him instead. The Bible tells us that Jesus was tempted in every way that we are. He understands what it feels like to be tempted to be afraid; but He also showed us that the way to freedom is through union and communion with the Father. Just like us, He went to the throne of grace to receive the strength He needed to overcome. We can see His example to us very clearly in Mark 14:32-34:

> *32 Then they went to a place called Gethsemane, and He said to His disciples, Sit down here while I pray. 33 And He took with Him Peter and James and John, and began to be struck with terror and amazement and deeply troubled and depressed. 34 And He said to them, My soul is exceedingly sad (overwhelmed with grief) so that it almost kills Me! Remain here and keep awake and be watching.* AMP

Jesus was tempted to be afraid. The Scriptures say His heart was stricken with terror, and gripped with fear. Just like us He felt depressed and deeply troubled. Knowing that Jesus felt the same way I feel at times encourages me and endears Him to my heart. Have you ever shared your heart with a good friend and were comforted realizing they felt the same way that you did? Jesus is your best friend and He can relate to the negative emotions your heart feels because He was tempted in the same ways that you are. He sympathizes with you. He truly understands what it feels like to be afraid, to the point of sweating great drops of blood.

Luke 22:44:

44And being in an agony he prayed more earnestly: and his sweat was as it were great drops of blood falling down to the ground. KJV

JESUS FELT AGONY FROM THE FEAR THAT GRIPPED HIS HEART, BUT HIS HEART WAS SET FREE THROUGH HIS UNION AND COMMUNION WITH HIS FATHER

Mark 14:35:

35And going a little farther, He fell on the ground and kept praying that if it were possible the [fatal] hour might pass from Him. 36And He was saying, Abba, [which means] Father, everything is possible for You. Take away this cup from Me; yet not what I will, but what You [will].

Jesus opened His heart and shared His fear with His Father. He was honest with Him about how He felt. Then He said, *"Abba Father, not what I will, but what you will."* He acknowledged His fear, but was willing to trust His Father completely because He knew His Father loved Him.

Mark 14:37:

> *37And He came back and found them sleeping, and He said to Peter, Simon, are you asleep? Have you not the strength to keep awake and watch [with Me for] one hour?*

If Jesus was tempted in every way that you are, how do you think Jesus felt when He realized that His friends had let Him down?

Mark 14:38:

> *38Keep awake and watch and pray [constantly], that you may not enter into temptation; the spirit indeed is willing, but the flesh is weak.*

Again we see Jesus sharing the secret to living a life free from sin. Prayer is not something we do just before we eat or for ten minutes in the morning during our devotional time. Prayer is a lifestyle of constant fellowship with the Father and the Son. It's not a religious duty, but an intimate relationship with the One Who loves us and meets all the needs of our heart. When we live in intimacy with Jesus, inviting Him into every facet of our hearts by sharing our fears, frustrations, doubts, and struggles with Him, He empowers us with His grace. In our weakness, He makes us strong (2 Corinthians 12:9).

Mark 14:39-50:

> *39He went away again and prayed, saying the same words. 40And again He came back and found them sleeping, for their eyes were very heavy; and they did not know what answer to give Him. 41And He came back a third time and said to them, Are you*

still sleeping and resting? It is enough [of that]! The hour has come. The Son of Man is betrayed into the hands of sinful men (men whose way or nature is to act in opposition to God). ⁴²Get up, let us be going! See, My betrayer is at hand!

⁴³And at once, while He was still speaking, Judas came, one of the Twelve [apostles], and with him a crowd of men with swords and clubs, [who came] from the chief priests and the scribes and the elders [of the Sanhedrin]. ⁴⁴Now the betrayer had given them a signal, saying, The One I shall kiss is [the Man]; seize Him and lead [Him] away safely [so as to prevent His escape]. ⁴⁵And when he came, he went up to Jesus immediately and said, Master! Master! and he embraced Him and kissed Him fervently. ⁴⁶And they threw their hands on Him and arrested Him.

⁴⁷But one of the bystanders drew his sword and struck the bond servant of the high priest and cut off his ear. ⁴⁸And Jesus said to them, Have you come out with swords and clubs as [you would] against a robber to capture Me? ⁴⁹I was with you daily in the temple [porches and courts] teaching, and you did not seize Me; but [this has happened] that the Scriptures might be fulfilled. AMP

JESUS KNEW WHERE TO GO WHEN HE WAS TEMPTED

Jesus ran to His Father who loved Him. He knew that it was only through His union and communion with His

Father that He would receive the strength He needed to carry out the Father's plan for His life. Although He went into the garden of Gethsemane feeling fearful and afraid, He came out empowered by the Holy Spirit. He was able to face His accusers fearlessly and fulfill the Father's plan for His life because His heart was filled with His Father's love.

Hebrews 12:2:

> *²Looking away [from all that will distract] to Jesus, Who is the Leader and the Source of our faith [giving the first incentive for our belief] and is also its Finisher [bringing it to maturity and perfection]. He, for the joy [of obtaining the prize] that was set before Him, endured the cross, despising and ignoring the shame, and is now seated at the right hand of the throne of God.* AMP

The Bible tells us that for the joy of obtaining the prize that was set before Him, Jesus endured the cross. His prize was being seated in the highest place of honor at the right hand of the Father and making it possible for us to be seated in Him. You and I are His prize, His treasured possession, and He wanted to be one with us.

In John 17:24 Jesus prayed:

> *²⁴"I desire that they also whom You have entrusted to Me [as Your gift to Me] may be with Me where I am, so that they may see My glory, which You have given Me [Your love gift to Me]; for You loved Me before the foundation of the world."* AMP

Wow! It was the desire of Jesus' heart that we would sit with Him in the highest place of honor. What love He demonstrated toward us to go through such agony and grief in order to give us such a priceless gift. He made it possible for all of us to live free from fear by bringing us into that same intimate relationship with Him and the Father.

Jesus was able to go to the cross fearlessly because He knew His Father's promise, and was secure in His Father's love. In John 17:24 He said, *"Father... You have loved me before the foundation of the world."* I often find myself following Jesus' example when I am faced with the temptation to fear or worry. I softly pray, *"Father, I know You love me because of the promises You've given me in Christ. I can rest in your great love!"*

You too, can live free from fear by living in the same relationship with the Father that Jesus did. Take the fears, frustrations, worries, concerns, and struggles of your heart to the Father. Live conscious of His love for you. Live in constant union and communion with Him and as you do, watch as the Holy Spirit empowers you to live fearlessly in this world.

Chapter 24

CAST YOUR CARES UPON JESUS

⁷Casting the whole of your care [all your anxieties,
all your worries, all your concerns,
once and for all] on Him,
for He cares for you affectionately
and cares about you watchfully.
1 PETER 5:7 AMP

The devil uses so many things in this world to tempt us to worry. Our finances, health, children, reputation, the state of the economy and our future are just a few of the things that can cause us concern. The devil knows that if we live in fear and worry, we won't be able to experience all that Jesus died to give us. Even though we're sons and daughters of the King, we are often tempted to live like fearful slaves.

Jesus came so that you could reign in this life like a king (Romans 5:17). He made it possible for you to live free from all worry and fear. Jesus loves you so much that He told you in His word to bring every care and concern of your heart to Him.

WHAT DOES IT MEAN TO CAST YOUR CARES UPON JESUS?

When you cast your cares upon Jesus, you give your cares to Him in prayer and you receive His promise into your heart. You share your concerns with Him and then begin to think upon what He says about your situation.

WHAT ARE SOME THINGS WE ARE TEMPTED TO WORRY ABOUT?

FEARS	GOD'S PROMISES
Finances	2 Corinthians 9:8; Matthew 6:25-33
Our children	Isaiah 54:13; Psalm 112:1-2; Proverbs 11:21
What others think of us	Psalm 139:14-18; Ephesians 1:4
Economy	Psalm 37:18-19
Protection	Psalm 91
Health	Proverbs 4:20-22
Decisions	Proverbs 16:3; Proverbs 3:5-6
Fear of failure	Psalm 1:1-3
Trials of life	Psalm 34:17-19

Not too long ago I was tempted to worry about a decision I needed to make. Rather than worry, I simply took my concern to the Lord in prayer and said, "Lord, I thank You that You promised to cause my thoughts to be agreeable to Your will so that my plans will prosper and succeed (Proverbs 16:3). I know You love me, Lord, and You lead me by Your Spirit." Almost immediately, my heart was filled with peace as I thought upon His promise to me and I was then able to make the necessary decision with perfect peace in my heart.

Philippians 4:6-9:

⁶Don't worry about anything; instead, pray about everything. Tell God what you need, and thank him for all he has done. ⁷Then you will experience God's peace, which exceeds anything we can understand. His peace will guard your hearts and minds as you live in Christ Jesus. ⁸And now, dear brothers and sisters, one final thing. Fix your thoughts on what is true, and honorable, and right, and pure, and lovely, and admirable. Think about things that are excellent and worthy of praise. ⁹Keep putting into practice all you learned and received from me—everything you heard from me and saw me doing. Then the God of peace will be with you. NLT ²

Isaiah 26:3:

³You keep in perfect peace all who trust in you, all whose thoughts are fixed on you. NLT ²

John 16:33:

³³I have told you these things so that in Me you may have [perfect] peace and confidence. In the world you will have tribulation and trials and distress and frustration; but be of good cheer [take courage; be confident; certain, undaunted]! For I have overcome the world. [I have deprived it of power to harm you and have conquered it for you.] AMP

Jesus speaks His promises to your heart so that you can have perfect peace and confidence in this world. There is no trial or temptation that you can face in this life that Jesus has not already overcome for you. He made you more than a conqueror through your union with Him. You can be joyful and confident because you are in Christ Jesus and every promise of God is *yes* and *amen* in your life. They cover every fear and concern of your heart. He has given you a promise of victory for every single problem you could ever face in this world. Because He already won the victory for you, all you need to do is rest in Him with a thankful heart.

RECEIVE HIS PROMISES WITH A THANKFUL HEART

1 Thessalonians 5:16-18:

> *¹⁶Be happy [in your faith] and rejoice and be gladhearted continually.... ¹⁷Be unceasing in prayer.... ¹⁸Thank [God] in everything [no matter what the circumstances may be, be thankful and give thanks], for this is the will of God for you [who are] in Christ Jesus. AMP*

Colossians 2:7:

> *⁷Let your roots grow down into him, and let your lives be built on him. Then your faith will grow strong in the truth you were taught, and you will overflow with thankfulness. NLT²*

Psalm 119:162:

> *¹⁶²I rejoice in your word like one who discovers a great treasure. NLT²*

The New Century Version of Psalm 119:162 says:

> *¹⁶²I am as happy over your promises as if I had found a great treasure.*

This verse brings to my mind all the endless treasures available to us in Christ Jesus. What joy we can live in when we keep our mind on the promises we have in Him.

Colossians 2:7 says that as your roots grow down into Jesus, your faith will grow strong in the truth, and your heart will overflow with thanksgiving. This is the kind of life that the Father wants you and me to live. He wants us to be happy in Jesus and receive His promises with a thankful heart. The Father created us to live in His love.

Psalm 50:23:

> *23He who brings an offering of praise and thanksgiving honors and glorifies Me...to him I will demonstrate the salvation of God. AMP*

According to *Lexical Aid to the New Testament*, the word *salvation* in this verse "is inclusive of all the blessings of God," which include every single promise Jesus has purchased for you. As you live in Jesus with a thankful heart, you'll experience the salvation of God in every area of your life.

Hebrews 6:17-19:

> *17God also bound Himself with an oath, so that those who received the promise could be perfectly sure that he would never change his mind. 18So God has given us both his promise and his oath. These two things are unchangeable because it is impossible for God to lie. Therefore, we who have fled to him for refuge can take new courage, for we can hold on to his promise with confidence. 19This confidence is like a strong and trustworthy anchor for our souls. NLT[1]*

Every one of us needs an anchor for our soul when we are faced with difficult situations. Each of the promises you have in Jesus are like a strong and trustworthy anchor for your soul. You can hold onto God's promise with confidence because God is completely trustworthy and it is impossible for Him to lie! Anytime you are tempted to worry or fear, you can run to your Heavenly Father and simply ask, "Father, what do You say about this situation in my life?" Every time He will remind you of who you are in Jesus and the promise you have in Him. He will give you His promise as an anchor for your soul. Through your union and communion with Him His love will be perfected in your heart. Cast your cares upon Him and you will live free from all fear as you live in His love.

PART 9

A PLACE OF REST

[14]I bow my knees before the Father of our Lord Jesus Christ.

[16]May He grant you out of the rich treasury of His glory to be strengthened and reinforced with mighty power in the inner man by the [Holy] Spirit [Himself indwelling your innermost being and personality]. [17]May Christ through your faith [actually] dwell (settle down, abide, make His permanent home) in your hearts! May you be rooted deep in love and founded securely on love, [18]that you may have the power and be strong to apprehend and grasp with all the saints [God's devoted people, the experience of that love] what is the breadth and length and height and depth [of it]; [19][that you may really come] to know [practically, through experience for yourselves] the love of Christ, which far surpasses mere knowledge [without experience]; that you may be filled [through all your being] unto all the fullness of God [may have the richest measure of the divine Presence, and become a body wholly filled and flooded with God Himself]!

[20]Now to Him Who, by (in consequence of) the [action of His] power that is at work within us, is able to [carry out His purpose and] do superabundantly, far over and above all that we [dare] ask or think [infinitely beyond our highest prayers, desires, thoughts, hopes, or dreams] — [21]To Him be glory in the church and in Christ Jesus throughout all generations forever and ever. Amen (so be it).

EPHESIANS 3:14, 16-21 AMP

Chapter 25

A LIFE LIVED IN TRUST

*[18] Why is my pain perpetual and my wound incurable,
refusing to be healed? Will you indeed be to me like a
deceitful brook, like waters that fail and are uncertain?
[19] Therefore thus says the Lord [to Jeremiah]: If you return
[and give up this mistaken tone of distrust and despair],
then I will give you again a settled place of quiet and
safety, and you will be My minister; and if you separate
the precious from the vile [cleansing your own heart from
unworthy and unwarranted suspicions concerning God's
faithfulness], you shall be My mouthpiece.... [20] And I will
make you to this people a fortified, bronze wall; they will
fight against you, but they will not prevail over you, for I
am with you to save and deliver you, says the Lord.
[21] And I will deliver you out of the hands of the wicked,
and I will redeem you.*

JEREMIAH 15:18-21: AMP

As children of God, He has promised us a place of
rest, where our hearts are free from fear and insecurity.
When we live in His love, we enter into His rest because
we trust Him completely. Unfortunately, many of God's
children never really experience this promise of rest. Even
after they've heard the Good News of God's love and
grace, they continue to live with condemnation, shame
and fear in their hearts. Wanting to understand why this
was the case I asked the Lord, "What keeps so many

of your children from really entering into Your rest and experiencing your promises in their lives?" What keeps them from experiencing the perfect and constant peace that you've promised them? Why is it that so many live with wounded hearts when you've promised to make them whole?" In response to my questions, the Holy Spirit led me to the previous passage of Scripture.

The prophet Jeremiah was facing a very dark time. Nothing seemed to be going the way he hoped. He found himself experiencing depression and disappointment within his soul and could not seem to find peace in his heart. So he asked, "Lord, why is my pain perpetual? Why is my heart not healed? Have You lied to me Lord? Are Your promises really true? Have You failed me?" His heart questioned God's faithfulness.

Have you ever been in a place in your life where you questioned God's promises? Where your circumstances didn't seem to be changing and you felt like God was far away? Has your heart ever asked these questions: *Lord, where are You?* or *Can I really trust You?*

You may have even heard the Good News that you are complete in Christ and that all of His promises to you are *Yes* and *Amen.* But you still find your heart saying, *I feel so incomplete. I lack in so many ways. It just sounds too good to be true.* The lies are somehow easier to believe because that is how your heart feels.

I remember back to a dark period in my own life when I questioned God's promises. My own personal failures and other people's negative experiences made me question the validity of God's Word. "Lord, where are you?" I found myself asking. "Do you even hear my prayers? Have you failed me? Can I really trust you? Is what you say about me really true?" Without my awareness, my mistaken tone of distrust created perpetual pain in my heart just like Jeremiah's. What I didn't realize was that my heart could not be healed as long as I questioned God's faithfulness.

WHAT IS THE SOLUTION TO THIS PERPETUAL PAIN?

The same answer God gave to Jeremiah is the one He gives to you and me: *If you'll return and give up this mistaken tone of distrust and despair then I will give you a place of rest and safety, and you will be my minister. If you'll separate the precious — the Truth — from the vile — the lies concerning my faithfulness — then you will stand strong in faith, and I will save and deliver you, says the Lord. [Author's Paraphrase]*

Through these verses it became very clear to me that the reason why so many of God's children never experience His promise of rest is because they won't let go of their questions concerning God's faithfulness. Instead of trusting Him and receiving the truth that would set their heart free, they hold onto the lies that have kept them in bondage their whole lives. The darkest moments of my life have been when my heart questioned the Good News. *Is what God says about me really true? Are His promises really true? It just doesn't seem to be working for me. Can I really trust God and His love for me?* From my own personal experience I can tell you that there's no greater pain for a believer than to carry a tone of distrust and unwarranted suspicions about God's faithfulness in your heart.

The devil's tactic is to use the negative circumstances in our lives to cause us to question God's love and faithfulness: a negative childhood experience, a divorce or bankruptcy, the loss of a child or business. He likes to taunt us with our failures, making us feel ashamed of our unanswered prayers, or unchanging negative circumstances. Even though we've all experienced disappointments in life, none of these things change the truth that God's word is true, He is faithful and trustworthy, and loves us completely!

Romans 8:35-37:

> [35] Can anything ever separate us from Christ's love? Does it mean he no longer loves us if we have trouble or calamity, or are persecuted, or hungry, or destitute, or in danger, or threatened with death? [36] (As the Scriptures say, "For your sake we are killed every day; we are being slaughtered like sheep.") [37] No, despite all these things, overwhelming victory is ours through Christ, who loved us. NLT [2]

I love how the Apostle Paul asks the question we have all wondered in our own hearts, and then confidently answers himself with the truth. Paul took the time to established his own heart in the truth of God's love and made the decision to trust Him even in the midst of difficult circumstances.

Any time I find my heart questioning God's faithfulness because of something I don't understand, the Holy Spirit always reminds me of one of my favorite Scriptures, and it always brings peace to my heart:

Proverbs 3:5-6:

> [5]*Trust in the LORD with all your heart and lean not on your own understanding;* [6] *in all your ways acknowledge him, and he will make your paths straight. NIV*

Every time I make the choice in my heart to trust the Lord completely, that is when I find true peace in my soul. When I let go of the lies my heart is tempted to believe and pray, "Heavenly Father, I choose to trust You! No matter how I feel or what I see, I trust that what You say is true," that is when I enter into that place of rest, and experience God's delivering power in my life.

One of the darkest times in my life was a few years back, when my husband went through a period of deep depression. During this time the devil attacked his mind and he became deeply depressed. I prayed for months that God would deliver him, but nothing seemed to be changing. Most days I was able to keep my eyes on Jesus, finding strength and hope in the promises I had in Him. But one particular day, after my husband had been battling this for months and it didn't look like my prayers were working at all, the devil came and attacked my mind with his lies. The enemy began to throw his fiery darts at my heart and his lies began to fill my thoughts. I began to question God's faithfulness. I questioned whether the Bible was really true. I even had this lie pass through my thoughts, *Are you sure there is even a God at all?* Darkness enveloped me as I pondered these suspicions about God and His faithfulness. My heart was filled with perpetual pain and I felt depressed and hopeless.

IN QUIETNESS AND IN [TRUSTING] CONFIDENCE SHALL BE YOUR STRENGTH

In the midst of this darkness, I remember turning to Jesus and asking for His grace to continue to trust Him. In response to my prayer the Holy Spirit reminded me of God's word in Isaiah 30:15:

> *15For thus said the Lord God, the Holy One of Israel: In returning [to Me] and resting [in] Me you shall be saved; in quietness and in [trusting] confidence shall be your strength. AMP*

I realized then that I had a choice to make within my own heart. I could either surrender these lies to the truth of my Heavenly Father's love and faithfulness and experience His strength and peace in my soul, or I could receive these lies as my truth and live in perpetual pain. Again the Holy Spirit spoke to my heart as He reminded me of Hebrews 10:35-36:

> *35Do not, therefore, fling away your fearless confidence, for it carries a great and glorious compensation of reward. 36For you have need of steadfast patience and endurance, so that you may perform and fully accomplish the will of God, and thus receive and carry away [and enjoy to the full] what is promised. AMP*

As God's grace filled my heart, I said, "Father, I choose to trust You! I know you love me and You are faithful!" As I separated the precious from the vile and gave up my suspicions about God's faithfulness, I found quietness and rest within my soul. In returning to Him and trusting Him with all my heart I found new strength. In the weeks to come I saw God deliver my husband from depression and fill his heart with joy once again. From out of that desperate place I experienced the delivering power of God and enjoyed to the full what He had promised.

By God's grace, every day and in every situation, I continue to choose to trust the Father's love and promises to me in Christ. That is where true freedom and rest in Christ is found.

You and I can live free from the perpetual pain in our hearts caused by questioning the truth of what Jesus really accomplished for us on the cross. If you want to live in the place of rest that God has promised you in Christ, give up any suspicions in your heart concerning God's love and faithfulness. Let go of the lies you've believed about God or yourself and acknowledge your choice to trust Him completely. 1 John 4:16 says, *We know how much God loves us and we have put our trust in His love.* NLT² When we come to Jesus and surrender all our doubts and fears to Him, that is when we truly live in a place of rest and experience His salvation in every area of our lives. As we learn to trust what He says completely, we will find ourselves truly living loved and living free!

Chapter 26

COME TO JESUS TO FIND REST

"Are you tired? Worn out? Burned out on religion? Come
to me. Get away with me and you'll recover your life. I'll
show you how to take a real rest. Walk with me and work
with me—watch how I do it. Learn the unforced rhythms
of grace. I won't lay anything heavy or ill-fitting on you.
Keep company with me and you'll learn to live
freely and lightly."

MATTHEW 11:28-30 MSG

In these verses we see Jesus inviting you to come and get away with Him and recover your life. He'll teach you how to truly rest, by trusting Him with all your heart. As you walk in intimacy with Jesus, you'll learn to live in His grace, freely and lightly. What a wonderful promise we have in Jesus!

Jesus demonstrated a heart that fully trusted in the love of His Father. In Mark 14:36 He prayed, *"Father... not what I will, but what You will,"* NKJV and in Luke 23:46, *"Father, I entrust my spirit into your hands."* NLT² During the most difficult moments of His life, He surrendered His opinions and His way of doing things, to the Father's. He knew that no matter how His heart felt at that moment, His Father was right and He could trust in His love!

As we make the daily decision to trust our Heavenly Father's love and opinion of us, we'll find true peace in our hearts. Like Jesus we can pray, "Father, I entrust my whole life to You. I trust what You say about me and know you have a good plan for my life." That's when we'll find true rest for our souls. Remember, your Heavenly Father loves you and His opinion of you is very good! His plan is to prosper you and give you a hope and a future. He is trustworthy and you can rest in Him.

Hebrews 4:1:

> *¹Therefore, while the promise of entering His rest still holds and is offered [today], let us be afraid [to distrust it], lest any of you should think he has come too late and has come short of [reaching] it.* AMP

The only thing that Scripture tells us to be afraid of is to distrust the promise of entering God's rest. The only true place of security in this world is in this place of rest that the Father has provided for us in Christ. When we trust the One Who loves us, we live safely and securely in His love.

Rest means:
- Freedom from anything that tires, troubles, or disturbs you
- To be free from care, worry, fear, and anxiety
- To have peace
- To trust and rely upon someone

When you've entered this promise of rest in Christ, you live free from anything that tires, troubles or disturbs you. You live free from stress, worry, and fear and experience perfect and constant peace as you trust and rely upon Jesus.

Hebrews 4:2-3 says:

> ²*For indeed we have had the glad tidings [Gospel*
> *of God] proclaimed to us just as truly as they [the*
> *Israelites of old did when the good news of deliverance*
> *from bondage came to them]; but the message they*
> *heard did not benefit them, because it was not mixed*
> *with faith (with the leaning of the entire personality*
> *on God in absolute trust and confidence in His*
> *power, wisdom, and goodness) by those who heard*
> *it; neither were they united in faith with the ones*
> *[Joshua and Caleb] who heard (did believe). ³For we*
> *who have believed (adhered to and trusted in and*
> *relied on God) do enter that rest.* AMP

We have had the Good News of the treasures available in Christ proclaimed to us just as the children of Israel did when the Good News of deliverance came to them; but God's promises didn't benefit them because they didn't believe that what God said about them was true.

God promised to deliver the Israelites and bring them into a land of abundance, where all their needs would be met and they would lack nothing. Because they had unwarranted suspicions of God's faithfulness in their hearts, they refused to trust Him. Instead, they chose to trust in their own ability and opinion of themselves. They saw themselves as grasshoppers instead of children of the King and it cost them dearly. Rather than enjoy the life of abundance God had promised them, they died in the wilderness (Hebrews 3:15-19).

Joshua and Caleb responded in a very different way to the Good News. They chose to believe what God said about them and fully trust in His power, wisdom, and goodness. They even tried to encourage the others to view themselves the way God saw them. "Believe what God says about you and He will bring you into this place of abundance just like He promised," they said. But the others refused to give up the lies they had chosen to believe about themselves, and God. As a result, they gave up their inheritance. Joshua and Caleb trusted in God's love and faithfulness, and as a result they and their children were able to enjoy to the full all that God had promised them.

THE GOOD NEWS IS THAT YOU HAVE BEEN MADE THE RIGHTEOUSNESS OF GOD IN CHRIST JESUS

All the promises and treasures in Christ are "Yes" and "Amen" in your life because of Jesus. You are no longer a fearful slave trying to earn God's blessing, but you are a son or daughter of the King and everything the Father has belongs to you. Jesus set you free from condemnation and shame. Your old sinful self was crucified with Christ and sin has lost its power in your life. Jesus gave you His honor and glory by making you one with Himself. You now sit in the highest place of honor in Christ. Your Heavenly Father declares you righteous, abundantly blessed, highly favored, and an heir to all His promised blessings because of your faith in Jesus. You are complete in Jesus and lack nothing! Your Heavenly Father's opinion of you is that you're very, very good and He rejoices over you with ecstatic delight. You enter into His rest by believing this Good News and enjoy your inheritance as a child of the King.

I must admit there have been times in the past when I responded to the Good News in the same way the children of Israel did, believing the lie that *I am not who God says I am*. This only served to cause perpetual pain in my heart and kept me in bondage to worry, insecurity, and sin. But there have been other times when I've responded like Joshua and Caleb, boldly declaring, "I am who my Father says I am in Jesus! I am the righteousness of God in Christ. I am loved and abundantly blessed because of Jesus!" When my heart agrees with the One Who loves me, I enter into His promise of rest, and partake of the treasures available to me in Jesus!

Hebrews 4:4-7:

> *⁴For in a certain place He has said this about the seventh day: And God rested on the seventh day from all His works. ⁵And [they forfeited their part in it, for] in this [passage] He said, They shall not enter My rest. ⁶Seeing then that the promise remains over [from past times] for some to enter that rest, and that those who formerly were given the good news about it and the opportunity, failed to appropriate it and did not enter because of disobedience, ⁷Again He sets a definite day, [a new] Today, [and gives another opportunity of securing that rest] saying through David after so long a time in the words already quoted, Today, if you would hear His voice and when you hear it, do not harden your hearts. AMP*

The children of Israel did not enter God's rest and forfeited their inheritance because they chose not to believe

God and instead held on to their own opinion and trusted in themselves. These verses warn us not to follow their example.

Every single day our Heavenly Father gives us the choice to trust Him or not to trust Him. Thank goodness that the promise of entering His rest is new every morning! Today when you hear Him speak to your heart and remind you of who you truly are in Jesus, don't harden your heart. Don't refuse the freedom He offers you by holding on to the enemy's lies and taking on your own opinion of yourself.

Hebrews 4:8-12:

> *[8][This mention of a rest was not a reference to their entering into Canaan.] For if Joshua had given them rest, He [God] would not speak afterward about another day. [9]So then, there is still awaiting a full and complete Sabbath-rest reserved for the [true] people of God; [10]For he who has once entered [God's] rest also has ceased from [the weariness and pain] of human labors, just as God rested from those labors peculiarly His own [11]Let us therefore be zealous and exert ourselves and strive diligently to enter that rest [of God, to know and experience it for ourselves], that no one may fail or perish by the same kind of unbelief and disobedience [into which those in the wilderness fell].[12]For the word that God speaks is alive and full of power [making it active, operative, energizing, and effective]. AMP*

Hebrews 4:12-13 in the Message Bible:

> *[12]God means what he says. What he says goes.*

His powerful Word is sharp as a surgeon's scalpel, cutting through everything, whether doubt or defense, laying us open to listen and obey. [13]Nothing and no one is impervious to God's Word. We can't get away from it—no matter what."

God means what He says, and what He says is the absolute truth and final authority in your life. His word is alive and full of power and you can trust completely in what He has to say about you! God has prepared a complete and total Sabbath rest for you and me. It is a place where we cease to try to be who God has already made us in Christ. It is a place where we cease to try to earn what we already have in Him. We rest in the finished work of Jesus! He's already taken care of everything that could ever concern you by making you an heir to all of God's promises. He is just waiting for you to accept His invitation to enter His rest. ***When you work, God rests, but when you rest, God works.*** As His power works in you, He is able to bring to pass His purpose in your life and do exceedingly abundantly above your highest prayers, desires, thoughts, hopes, and dreams.

God has a place of rest for you to live every day. He has made it possible for you to live free from worry and fear, simply by trusting in His great love. Believe what He says about you in Christ. Say "Amen!" to His promises. Trust Him completely with your life and just like Joshua and Caleb, you'll live in that place of abundance that Jesus has prepared for you. As you come to Jesus, you'll find rest for your soul, and you'll experience the wonderful inheritance you have in Him!

Chapter 27

GRACE: THE POWER TO BELIEVE

14Inasmuch as we have a great High Priest Who has [already] ascended and passed through the heavens, Jesus the Son of God, let us hold fast to our confession [of faith in Him]. 15For we do not have a High Priest Who is unable to understand and sympathize and have a shared feeling with our weaknesses and infirmities and liability to the assaults of temptation, but One Who has been tempted in every respect as we are, yet without sinning. 16Let us then fearlessly, and confidently and boldly draw near to the throne of grace (the throne of God's unmerited favor to us sinners), that we may receive mercy [for our failures] and find grace to help in good time for every need [appropriate help and well-timed help, coming just when we need it].

HEBREWS 4:14-16 AMP

In the last chapter, we read Hebrews 4:1-13 where we learned about the promise of rest we have in Jesus. We enter this rest as our hearts believe the truth of who we truly are in Christ.

But our Heavenly Father knows all too well that the enemy of our souls works overtime to convince our hearts of the lie: "You're not who God says you are." He knows we are continually tempted to believe this lie, so by His grace He has given us the power to overcome this temptation and believe Him instead.

Have you ever doubted your new identity in Jesus? Have

you ever been tempted to believe the devil's lies instead of the truth? Verse 15 says that Jesus was tempted just like you and I, to question His identity as the Father's Son. He was tempted in every way that we are, yet He did not give in to the devil's lies. This truth comforts my heart to know that Jesus understands my temptation at times to believe the devil's lies. I have felt weak in faith during moments when my circumstances were screaming, *What God says about you is not true!* Yet, I have found strength to believe my Heavenly Father and rest in His love when I come to His throne of grace.

WHERE CAN YOU FIND THE STRENGTH TO TRUST, WHEN YOU FEEL WEAK IN FAITH?

We find the strength to believe at the throne of grace. The power to believe is found in keeping our eyes on Jesus. As we turn to Him in our moments of weakness, He strengthens us with the power to believe who we are in Him.

Hebrews 12:1-2:

> *¹Therefore, since we are surrounded by such a huge crowd of witnesses to the life of faith, let us strip off every weight that slows us down, especially the sin that so easily trips us up. And let us run with endurance the race God has set before us. ²We do this by keeping our eyes on Jesus, the champion who initiates and perfects our faith."* NLT²

Hebrews chapter 11 is full of examples of people who chose to believe God in the face of very difficult circumstances. They chose to believe what God said about them instead of the enemy's lies. These people are the *huge crowd of witnesses to the life of faith* that verse 1 is talking about.

Jesus is the author and finisher of our faith, and He lives in you and me. As we keep our eyes on Him, He creates within us the faith to believe, and He also brings it to perfection. He creates in us the desire and the power to completely trust Him (Philippians 2:13).

Romans 10:17:

> [17] *Faith comes from listening to this message of good news — the Good News about Christ.* NLT [1]

Few versions of the Bible translate Galatians 2:20 exactly as it appears in the original Greek. Paul wrote: *I am crucified with Christ: nevertheless I live; yet not I, but Christ liveth in me: and the life which I now live in the flesh I live by the faith of the Son of God, who loved me, and gave himself for me.* KJV

Most translations read, *I live by faith in the Son of God.* Yet the power of this verse is found in the truth that we live *by the faith of the Son of God.* We live by the very same faith that Jesus had in His Father's love. Jesus said only what He heard His Father say about Him, and in His moment of weakness He found strength in His Father's love. If Jesus lives in us then we have the exact same ability to believe the truth as He does because we are one with Him. Paul is saying that he doesn't depend on his own faith, but the faith of Jesus, the One Who loved him and gave himself for him.

Your old life ended when it was crucified with Christ. Your old nature, which lived in doubt and unbelief, died with Jesus. That's not who you are anymore. Your new nature is filled with the very faith of Jesus. He empowers you with His faith to believe the Father's love and embrace your true identity in Him.

When you find yourself struggling to believe God, remember that you live not by your own faith, but by the faith of Jesus. He loves you and gave Himself for you so that you could be completely one with Him. In your weakness, He makes you strong!

You lack nothing in Christ! You are complete in Him! You have His ability to trust the Father's love. You don't have to try anymore to have enough faith, simply rest in Jesus. He covered it all for you!

PART 10

ETERNAL LOVE

*¹⁷I pray that Christ will be more and more at home
in your hearts as you trust in him. May your roots
go down deep into the soil of God's marvelous love.
¹⁸And may you have the power to understand, as
all God's people should, how wide, how long, how
high, and how deep his love really is. ¹⁹May you
experience the love of Christ, though it is so great
you will never fully understand it. Then you will
be filled with the fullness of life and power
that comes from God!*

*²⁰Now glory be to God! By His mighty power at
work within us, he is able to accomplish infinitely
more than we would ever dare to ask or hope.
²¹May he be given glory in the church and in Christ
Jesus forever and ever."*

EPHESIANS 3:17-21 NLT [1]

Chapter 28

THE GREATEST PROMISE OF ALL!

¹The LORD is my shepherd; I have all that I need.
²He lets me rest in green meadows;
he leads me beside peaceful streams.
³He renews my strength. He guides me along
right paths, bringing honor to his name
⁴Even when I walk through the darkest valley,
I will not be afraid, for you are close beside me.
Your rod and your staff protect and comfort me.
⁵You prepare a feast for me in the presence of my enemies.
You honor me by anointing my head with oil.
My cup overflows with blessings.
⁶Surely your goodness and unfailing love
will pursue me all the days of my life,
and I will live in the house of the LORD forever.

PSALM 23 NLT[2]

As you learn to live loved by your Heavenly Father you will grow in your understanding of what Jesus really accomplished for you on the cross. The more you receive the truth in your heart the more freedom you will walk in. As you come to know Jesus more intimately, your heart will become more established in the truth of who you truly are in Him and you'll begin enjoying the endless treasures available to you in Jesus. You've learned from Romans 8:39 that the love of God is revealed in each promise you have in Jesus. Every promise is a revelation of His love. As you receive His promises in your heart by agreeing with the One Who loves you, your roots will go down deep into the soil of His marvelous love.

David was a man who grew in the understanding of God's love. The Bible tells us that God himself called David a man after God's own heart (1 Samuel 13:13-14). Psalm 23 shows us the intimacy David had with God, and that he was living loved at the time he wrote it. As David renewed his mind to the truth and talked to His Savior about God's promises to him, David's heart was established in God's love. Psalm 23 shows us how David responded to Jesus.

I love this passage of Scripture; it clearly shows the peace we can live in as we walk this life journey with Jesus. We can live loved by Him, remembering that in Christ we lack nothing! He gives us peace and leads us in paths of righteousness.

No matter what trial we may face, we can live free from fear just like David did, by reminding ourselves of His promises to us. Surely His goodness and unfailing love will pursue us all the days of our lives, and we will live with Him forever!

WHEN JESUS DIED AND ROSE AGAIN, HE OVERCAME EVERY TRIAL WE COULD EVER FACE IN THIS LIFE. HE BECAME OUR CONQUERING KING

In John 16:33 Jesus said:

> 33*I have told you these things, so that in Me you may have [perfect] peace and confidence. In the world you have tribulation and trials and distress and frustration; but be of good cheer [take courage;*

be confident, certain, undaunted]! For I have overcome the world. [I have deprived it of power to harm you and have conquered it for you.] AMP

I often think of this verse when I face a difficult situation in my life. It reminds me that Jesus overcame the world for me and deprived sin of its power to harm me. He gave us His great and precious promises so that we could escape this world's corruption and partake of His divine nature (2 Peter 1:4). He speaks His promises to our hearts so that you and I can have perfect peace and confidence in the midst of every negative circumstance that we face. In Christ, God has given us so many precious promises for our life here on this earth.

But the greatest promise of all is spending eternity with Jesus. He comforts us by promising that even though we are faced with trials and temptations in this life, one day we will live free from them all! There will be no more trials, no more temptations, no more distresses, and no more frustrations. Every one of us as a son or daughter of God, will live in the ultimate freedom Jesus paid to give us through the cross. As Psalm 23:6 says, *I will live in the house of the Lord forever!* Although the average American lifespan is now seventy-eight years, the Bible tells us that our lives here are just a vapor and a wisp (James 4:14). Eternity, on the other hand, will last forever, and Jesus has promised that we will spend it with Him and those we love, in a place beyond anything we could ever imagine.

Surely His goodness and unfailing love will pursue us all the days of our lives and we will dwell with Him forever!

Jesus took our sin and judgment upon Himself on the cross so we could share with Him in the riches available to us in Christ. He loves us so much He made each of us an heir of God's blessings here on earth and for all eternity!

Colossians 3:1-2:

> *[1] Since you have been raised to a new life with Christ, set your sights on the realities of heaven, where Christ sits at God's right hand in the place of honor and power. [2] Let heaven fill your thoughts. Do not think only about things down here on earth.*
>
> *NLT[1]*

In my journey of living loved, my Heavenly Father has given me a glimpse into the place where you and I will spend eternity. My thoughts used to be completely focused on this earth. Lately I find myself longing for the day when I'll see my Savior face-to-face; when all of life's questions and challenges will be gone, and I will finally arrive at the place He has destined for you and me all along. The Bible tells us that we are foreigners in this land (Hebrews 11:8-10); we are simply passing through this life, heading toward our ultimate destination with Jesus! This earth is not our home; we're on a mission trip, here to learn to live loved and share God's love with others. We are here to tell of God's amazing grace and to invite others to journey with us to the place Jesus has prepared for those who put their trust in Him.

In this promise of eternity with Him, we once again see the height, and depth of Jesus' great love for us.

2 Corinthians 4:15-18:

> *15...as God's grace reaches more and more people, there will be great thanksgiving, and God will receive more and more glory. 16That is why we never give up. Though our bodies are dying, our spirits are being renewed every day. 17For our present troubles are small and won't last very long. Yet they produce for us a glory that vastly outweighs them and will last forever! 18So we don't look at the troubles we can see now; rather, we fix our gaze on things that cannot be seen. For the things we see now will soon be gone, but the things we cannot see will last forever. NLT 2*

As greater numbers of people hear of our Savior's amazing love and grace, there will be great thanksgiving in the hearts of God's children as His glory shines brighter in this world. Our present trials won't last long, but His glory will last forever! Let us fix our eyes on Jesus and all that He has prepared for us. This present world will soon be gone, but the place He has prepared for us will be far more beautiful than any other place our eyes have seen.

JESUS DIED ON THE CROSS TO GIVE YOU THE PROMISE OF ETERNAL LIFE

If Jesus should tarry, your body will die, but the real you will live forever! He has qualified you by making you righteous so that you can live in the most wonderful place you could ever imagine — spending eternity with Jesus is the greatest promise of all!

Chapter 29

I GO TO PREPARE A PLACE FOR YOU

*"¹Don't let your hearts be troubled. Trust in God, and
trust also in me. ²There is more than enough room in
my Father's home. If this were not so, would I have told
you that I am going to prepare a place for you? ³When
everything is ready, I will come and get you, so that you
will always be with me where I am. ⁴And you know the
way to where I am going." ⁵"No, we don't know, Lord,"
Thomas said. "We have no idea where you are going, so
how can we know the way?" ⁶Jesus told him, "I am the
way, the truth, and the life. No one can come to
the Father except through me.*

JOHN 14:1-6 NLT²

In the last chapter we learned that the greatest promise
ever given in Christ is that we who have placed our faith in
Him, will never truly die. Even though your earthly body
will die, the real you will continue to live for all eternity.
Because of His great love, Jesus has prepared an amazing
place for you and me to live with Him forever.

Jesus told us that He is the way, the truth and the life.
The only way to this place is through trusting Him. John
3:16 says, *"For God loved the world so much that he gave his
one and only Son, so that everyone who believes in him will not
perish but have eternal life." NLT²*

What is this place that He has prepared for us like? Let's
look in Scripture to discover the most wonderful place
your heart can imagine.

Revelation 21:1-7; 10, 11, 21-27:

> [1] *Then I saw a new heaven and a new earth, for the old heaven and the old earth had disappeared. And the sea was also gone. [2] And I saw the holy city, the new Jerusalem, coming down from God out of heaven like a bride beautifully dressed for her husband. [3] I heard a loud shout from the throne, saying, "Look, God's home is now among his people! He will live with them, and they will be his people. God himself will be with them. [4] He will wipe every tear from their eyes, and there will be no more death or sorrow or crying or pain. For the old world and its evils are gone forever." NLT [1]*

> [5] *And the one sitting on the throne said, "Look, I am making everything new!" And then he said to me, "Write this down, for what I tell you is trustworthy and true." [6] And he also said, "It is finished! I am the Alpha and the Omega—the Beginning and the End. To all who are thirsty I will give freely from the springs of the water of life. [7] All who are victorious will inherit all these blessings, and I will be their God, and they will be my children.*

> [10] *So he took me in the Spirit to a great, high mountain, and he showed me the holy city, Jerusalem, descending out of heaven from God. [11] It shone with the glory of God and sparkled like a precious stone—like jasper as clear as crystal.*

> [21] *The twelve gates were made of pearls—each gate*

from a single pearl! And the main street was pure gold, as clear as glass. ²²*I saw no temple in the city, for the Lord God Almighty and the Lamb are its temple.* ²³*And the city has no need of sun or moon, for the glory of God illuminates the city, and the Lamb is its light.* ²⁴*The nations will walk in its light, and the kings of the world will enter the city in all their glory.* ²⁵*Its gates will never be closed at the end of day because there is no night there.* ²⁶*And all the nations will bring their glory and honor into the city.* ²⁷*Nothing evil will be allowed to enter, nor anyone who practices shameful idolatry and dishonesty—but only those whose names are written in the Lamb's Book of Life.* NLT²

1 John 5:4-5:

> ⁴*For whatever is born of God is victorious over the world; and this is the victory that conquers the world, even our faith.* ⁵*Who is it that is victorious over [that conquers] the world but he who believes that Jesus is the Son of God [who adheres to, trusts in, and relies on that fact]?* AMP

In this wonderful place there will be no more crying, and people's hearts will never be hurt or broken again. The people we love will never die and no one will ever be sad or depressed. There will be no more poverty, no more lack; no more sickness and no more pain. All the trials, challenges, worries, and fears which come at us in this world will be gone. The old world and everything evil in it will be gone forever!

The Holy City is absolutely beautiful! The glory of God shines in every place. Prosperity is everywhere. Everyone is abundantly prosperous as they walk on streets of gold and live in the most beautiful homes. Everyone will walk in divine health for all eternity! The hearts of God's people will only feel love, joy and peace forever! Nothing evil will be allowed to enter, but only we whose names are written in the Lamb's book of life. What a promise of love our Savior purchased for each one of us!

Revelation 22:1-6, 20-21:

> *¹Then the angel showed me a river with the water of life, clear as crystal, flowing from the throne of God and of the Lamb. ²It flowed down the center of the main street. On each side of the river grew a tree of life, bearing twelve crops of fruit, with a fresh crop each month. The leaves were used for medicine to heal the nations. ³No longer will there be a curse upon anything. For the throne of God and of the Lamb will be there, and his servants will worship him. ⁴And they will see his face, and his name will be written on their foreheads. ⁵And there will be no night there—no need for lamps or sun—for the Lord God will shine on them. And they will reign forever and ever.*
>
> *⁶Then the angel said to me, "Everything you have heard and seen is trustworthy and true. The Lord God, who inspires his prophets, has sent his angel to tell his servants what will happen soon. ²⁰He*

*who is the faithful witness to all these things says,
"Yes, I am coming soon!" Amen! Come, Lord Jesus!
²¹May the grace of the Lord Jesus be with God's holy
people. NLT²*

In this glorious land there will no longer be a curse
on anything. The Bible says the earth we live in now is
cursed because of sin. That is why we see mosquitoes, flies
and pestilence; why people grow old and everything man
builds eventually wears out and needs repair. There are
floods, earthquakes, and tornados that bring great death
and destruction because of the curse that is on the earth.
The Bible tells us that the earth itself is actually groaning
for its complete redemption. Jesus is going to create a new
heaven and a new earth where nothing grows old or wears
out; where everything stays beautiful forever! In fact, a
river of life flows through the city and the tree of life will
have the most delicious fruit. Jesus promises us that we
will reign forever with Him in this most amazing place!

In the last two verses of the Bible. Jesus promised, *"Yes,
I am coming soon!"*

As I read about this glorious place He has prepared for
all of us and gain a deeper understanding of His amazing
love, I find my heart responding to Him by saying, *"Come
Lord Jesus! Come quickly!"*

Hebrews 9:24-28:

*²⁴For Christ did not enter into a holy place made
with human hands, which was only a copy of the
true one in heaven. He entered into heaven itself*

> *to appear now before God on our behalf.* ²⁵*And he did not enter heaven to offer himself again and again, like the high priest here on earth who enters the Most Holy Place year after year with the blood of an animal.* ²⁶*If that had been necessary, Christ would have had to die again and again, ever since the world began. But now, once for all time, he has appeared at the end of the age to remove sin by his own death as a sacrifice.* ²⁷*And just as each person is destined to die once and after that comes judgment,* ²⁸*so also Christ died once for all time as a sacrifice to take away the sins of many people. He will come again, not to deal with our sins, but to bring salvation to all who are eagerly waiting for him.* NLT²

These verses clearly reveal that when Jesus comes back, He is not coming to deal with our sins, but to completely save us from the evils of this world. He is coming to bring complete redemption and salvation to those of us who are waiting for Him.

Hebrews 9:28:
> ²⁸*Christ died once for all time as a sacrifice to take away the sins of many people.*

Hebrews 10:14:
> ¹⁴*For by that one offering he forever made perfect those who are being made holy.* NLT²

YOU AND I HAVE BEEN MADE PERFECT FOREVER
THROUGH JESUS' ONE SACRIFICE

When we stand before the judgment seat of Christ, we will be judged righteous in Jesus because of our faith in Him.

Jude 1:24:

24Now to Him Who is able to keep you without stumbling or slipping or falling, and to present [you] unblemished (blameless and faultless) before the presence of His glory in triumphant joy and exultation [with unspeakable, ecstatic delight]. AMP

Remember the courtroom scene? When you stand before Him, you will hear Him say with triumphant joy, "My beloved, you are perfect, innocent, justified, and righteous because you placed your faith in My Son Jesus'sacrifice for you. I am fully pleased with you because of your faith in Him."

Let's look at one more passage of Scripture that reveals the wonderful place that Jesus has made ready for us to live in:

Isaiah 11:6-10, 13:

6In that day the wolf and the lamb will live together; the leopard and the goat will be at peace. Calves and yearlings will be safe among lions, and the little child will lead them all. 7The cattle will graze among bears. Cubs and calves will lie down together. And lions will eat grass as the livestock do. 8Babies will crawl safely among poisonous snakes.

Yes, a little child will put its hand in a nest of deadly snakes and pull it out unharmed. ⁹Nothing will hurt or destroy in all my holy mountain. And as the waters fill the sea, so the earth will be filled with people who know the LORD. ¹⁰In that day the heir to David's throne will be a banner of salvation to all the world. The nations will rally to him, for the land where he lives will be a glorious place. NLT¹

¹³Then at last the jealousy between Israel and Judah will end. They will not fight against each other anymore. NLT¹

What a beautiful picture of perfect peace and love among all people. There will be no more killing or wars; it will be a place of perfect safety. Mothers won't have to worry about their babies; they will be raised in a perfect world, without sin, or harm. This land in which we will live with Jesus forever, will be a glorious place! When I think about this eternal home Jesus has prepared for us, I am once again overwhelmed with His great love. One day we will see Jesus — the One Who loves us completely — and it will be so glorious, so amazing, and so beyond anything our hearts could ever think, desire, hope, dream or imagine, and we will live with Him there, forever!

Chapter 30

DEATH IS SWALLOWED UP IN VICTORY

[42] It is the same way for the resurrection of the dead. Our earthly bodies, which die and decay, will be different when they are resurrected, for they will never die. [43] Our bodies now disappoint us, but when they are raised, they will be full of glory. They are weak now, but when they are raised, they will be full of power. [48] Every human being has an earthly body just like Adam's, but our heavenly bodies will be just like Christ's. [50] What I am saying, dear brothers and sisters, is that flesh and blood cannot inherit the Kingdom of God. These perishable bodies of ours are not able to live forever. [51] But let me tell you a wonderful secret God has revealed to us. Not all of us will die, but we will all be transformed. [52] It will happen in a moment, in the blinking of an eye, when the last trumpet is blown. For when the trumpet sounds, the Christians who have died will be raised with transformed bodies. And then we who are living will be transformed so that we will never die. [54] When this happens — when our perishable earthly bodies have been transformed into heavenly bodies that will never die — then at last the Scripture will come true: "Death is swallowed up in victory. [55] O death, where is your victory? O death, where is your sting?" [56] For sin is the sting that results in death, and the law gives sin its power. [57] How we thank God, who gives us victory over sin and death through Jesus Christ our Lord!

1 CORINTHIANS 15:42-43, 48, 50-52, 54-57: NLT [1]

As we learn to live in the Father's love, we can have peace in every situation. In His great love for us, Jesus won us the ultimate victory.

WE WIN BECAUSE OF JESUS!

Death is swallowed up in complete victory. We win because of Jesus; we win no matter what! I remember a particular instance in my life when I was believing God for a person to live and not die, but they died anyway. I was so discouraged about the outcome and felt so defeated. I remember saying, "Lord, it's not fair. I don't understand. It feels like the devil has won." I was feeling perpetual pain in my heart because I questioned God's faithfulness. So, I took my heart to Jesus and said, "Lord, please show me Your perspective on this. Show me the truth that will set my heart free so I can completely trust You." Then the Holy Spirit led me to read 1 Corinthians chapter fifteen. He then spoke to my heart from these verses, "Connie, you see death as a defeat, but I have swallowed death up in complete victory." It was at this moment, that my perspective began to change. I realized that death cannot defeat us. We win because of Jesus. I began to see this person in heaven: happy, healed, whole, and completely free! I thought, *Wow, there is no defeat in death.* There is only complete and total victory!

Isaiah 57:1-2:

> *¹The righteous pass away; the godly often die before their time. No one seems to ... understand that God*

is protecting them from the evil to come. ²For the godly who die will rest in peace. NLT¹

The Hebrew word for peace in this verse, is *shalom* *[Strongs H7965].* According to the Strong's Concordance it means "safe, well, happy; health, prosperity, and peace." These Scriptures have given me such peace because I now truly understand that the people I love who have died are not dead at all. They are very much alive in Christ. Sickness and death did not win because they are in heaven with Jesus. They are experiencing the glory of God. From now into all eternity, they will experience perfect health and perfect peace! Praise You, Jesus!

Understanding this has given me a deeper revelation of God's amazing love, and strengthened me to trust Him even more. I don't have to fear disappointment or defeat. Those of us who place our faith in Christ can never be defeated. We can completely trust Jesus to live in divine health as we walk upon this earth, because either way we win! Divine health is our eternal inheritance, purchased by Jesus for us on the cross. We live loved by accepting the truth that by His stripes we are healed! I am constantly renewing my mind to the truth that I am the righteousness of God in Christ Jesus and sickness has no right in my body. Divine health is my inheritance in Christ Jesus. I have chosen to continue believing God's promise to me until I take my last breath, because I know that the real you and the real me are healed and whole in Jesus. Our Heavenly Father has given us the victory over sin and death through our Lord Jesus Christ!

1 Thessalonians 4:13-14:

¹³And now, dear brothers and sisters, we want you to know what will happen to the believers who have died so you will not grieve like people who have no hope. ¹⁴For since we believe that Jesus died and was raised to life again, we also believe that when Jesus returns, God will bring back with him the believers who have died. NLT²

We can celebrate the lives of those we love who have died before us, because they are still very much alive with Jesus. They've finished their mission trip and have gone home to the most glorious place we could ever imagine. And when we finish our mission trip, we will be with them forever. Although we do grieve when we lose someone we love, we do not grieve like the world because we have hope beyond this life. What a wonderful promise we have in Jesus!

The Apostle Paul, who prayed that we might know the love of Christ and be filled with the fullness of God, said in Philippians 1:21-25:

²¹For to me, living means living for Christ, and dying is even better. ²²But if I live, I can do more fruitful work for Christ. So I really don't know which is better. ²³I'm torn between two desires: I long to go and be with Christ, which would be far better for me. ²⁴But for your sakes, it is better that I continue to live. ²⁵Knowing this, I am convinced that I will remain alive so I can continue to help all of you grow and experience the joy of your faith. NLT²

The Apostle Paul, who had once hated Christians, had a revelation of the love of Christ. Although he greatly desired to be with Jesus in eternity, he knew he had not completed his mission trip here on earth. The great love Paul had experienced compelled him to complete his earthly journey with Jesus, sharing the Good News of God's love and grace with the people around him to help them grow in their faith.

PERFECT LOVE CASTS OUT ALL FEAR OF DEATH

Hebrews 2:9-15:

> [9] *What we do see is Jesus, who was given a position "a little lower than the angels"; and because he suffered death for us, he is now "crowned with glory and honor." Yes, by God's grace, Jesus tasted death for everyone.* [10] *God, for whom and through whom everything was made, chose to bring many children into glory. And it was only right that he should make Jesus, through his suffering, a perfect leader, fit to bring them into their salvation.* [11] *So now Jesus and the ones he makes holy have the same Father. That is why Jesus is not ashamed to call them his brothers and sisters.* [12] *For he said to God, "I will proclaim your name to my brothers and sisters. I will praise you among your assembled people."* [13] *He also said, "I will put my trust in him," that is, "I and the children God has given me."* [14] *Because God's children are human beings—made of flesh and blood—the Son also became flesh and blood. For only as a human being could he die, and only*

by dying could he break the power of the devil, who had the power of death. [15] Only in this way could he set free all who have lived their lives as slaves to the fear of dying. NLT[2]

Jesus loves us so much that He suffered death for you and me on the cross. Because He did this, He sits next to the Father in heaven crowned with glory and honor. The Father's plan has always been to bring you and me into this same glorious position in Christ, by making us one with Himself. We are His beloved children and we can share the same intimacy with the Father that Jesus does, as we live loved by Him. Jesus even freed us from the fear of death. When He tasted death for us, He gave us the gift of eternal life. We can enjoy our Heavenly Father's blessing upon our lives on the earth, and for all eternity, because of His great love!

Just like the Apostle Paul, we can confidently and boldly say:

[38]"I am convinced that nothing can ever separate me from God's love. Neither death nor life, neither angels nor demons, neither my fears for today nor my worries about tomorrow—not even the powers of hell can separate me from God's love. [39] No power in the sky above or in the earth below—indeed, nothing in all creation will ever be able to separate me from the love of God that is revealed in Christ Jesus my Lord."

ROMANS 8:38-39 NLT[2] (AUTHOR'S PARAPHRASE)

BIBLIOGRAPHY

Holy Bible Special Hebrew-Greek Key Study Edition
copyright © 1984 by Spiros Zodhiates and AMG International, Inc.

Strong's Exhaustive Concordance of the Bible

Merriam Webster's College Dictionary, 10th Edition
copyright © 1994 by Merriam-Webster, Inc.

Thorndike Barnhart Intermediate Dictionary

[1]Reference: http://www.christiananswers.net/dictionary/justification.html:
Bible Encyclopedia

ABOUT THE AUTHOR

Connie Witter is a speaker, author, and Bible Study teacher. Her best-selling book, *P.S. God Loves You*, has sold over 150,000 copies. She is the founder of *Because of Jesus Ministries* which was established in 2006 and has been teaching Ladies Bible Studies for over 15 years. Her ground-breaking Bible Study, *Because of Jesus*, was published in 2002 and is the foundation of her life and ministry. Since 2005, she has held an annual *Because of Jesus Conference* in Tulsa and the outlying areas. In addition to writing Bible Studies, Connie has traveled throughout the United States and Russia, sharing the life changing message of *Because of Jesus*. She has been the guest speaker at Women's Conferences, ladies retreats and meetings, and has also spoken into the lives of teenage girls. She has also been a guest on several Christian TV and radio programs, and has had her own weekly TV program, *Because of Jesus*. Her online Bible Studies can be seen worldwide through her ministry website, *www.becauseofJesus.com*. Each week she shares the Good News: that we are righteous, valuable, precious, blessed, favored and extravagantly loved by God, because of Jesus. Thousands of lives have been changed through her ministry.

If you are interested in having Connie come speak at your event, you can contact her at:

Connie@becauseofJesus.com

BIBLE STUDIES BY CONNIE WITTER

Because of Jesus
Living Loved, Living Free
Awake to Righteousness
The Lord is My Shepherd: Psalm 23

CD/DVD SERIES BY CONNIE WITTER

Because of Jesus
Living Loved, Living Free
Awake to Righteousness
The Lord is My Shepherd: Psalm 23

OTHER BOOKS BY CONNIE WITTER

P.S. God Loves You
21 Days to Discover Who You Are in Jesus
The Inside Story Teen Devotional
The Inside Story for Girls Devotional
Yes I Am! Preschool Curriculum

You can purchase any of these resources at:

BecauseofJesus.com

We would love to hear how this book has impacted your life.
To contact the author, write:
Connie Witter
Because of Jesus Ministries
P.O. Box 3064
Broken Arrow, OK 74013
Connie@becauseofJesus.com
For additional copies of this book go to:
www.becauseofJesus.com
Or call 918-994-6500